CATHOLIC ETHICS
AND PROTESTANT ETHICS

CATHOLIC ETHICS
AND
PROTESTANT ETHICS

by

Roger Mehl

TRANSLATED BY JAMES H. FARLEY

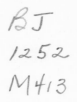

THE WESTMINSTER PRESS
Philadelphia

Translation of
Éthique catholique et éthique protestante
© 1970 by Delachaux & Niestlé
Neuchâtel, Switzerland

The Warfield Lectures
Princeton Theological Seminary
1968

ISBN 0–664–20903–3

LIBRARY OF CONGRESS CATALOG CARD No. 73–141511

Book design by Dorothy Alden Smith

Published by The Westminster Press®
Philadelphia, Pennsylvania

PRINTED IN THE UNITED STATES OF AMERICA

To James I. McCord
President of Princeton Theological Seminary

CONTENTS

INTRODUCTION

I would like, first of all, to make some comments about the spirit of our enterprise. We shall not be concerned with controversy or with apologetic. But this general statement calls for some explanations. For one thing, to reject controversy is not to reject discussion or to prohibit criticism. Controversy is rooted in apologetic. It is something that we find in a person whose positions are so assured that his only concern is to put another person in a difficult position and to win out over him. Discussion, on the other hand, seeks to go back to first principles and, on the basis of these principles, to understand what is common behind the reasons for divergence. It is this comprehension that permits one to distinguish discussion from controversy. Controversy always postulates error, heresy, and bad faith on the part of the other. It ceases only when it feels that this error, heresy, and bad faith have been clearly established.

At this point, I might make a parenthetical observation: we ordinarily speak of discussion today in terms of "dialogue," but this word, despite its richness of meaning and its relationship to Socratic dialectic, is beginning to lose its savor, since it is used to describe every meeting of ecclesiastical dignitaries.

In any event, discussion seeks not to rend but to comprehend. That is, it seeks to go beyond doctrinal formulations and to grasp the intention that is expressed in such formulations. It seeks to justify this intention or at least to recognize the legitimate aspects of this intention. It does so, of course, at the risk of calling into question the manner in which the intention is explicated and the consequences which this explication has entailed. Discussion is possible only among men of good faith, and good faith presupposes a basic accord, an accord at the level of intentions. But this accord is possible only if we admit that, in principle, we may possibly learn something from the other, only if we admit that the position of the other can become a question for us. The reciprocity of this calling-into-question is what characterizes discussion. And once this reciprocity is present, it is no longer possible to engage in apologetic, that is, in a *pro domo* intellectual assault which is intended to confuse and vanquish the other. Apologetic presupposes a consciousness of one's own superiority, so that the persons involved no longer stand in a relationship of equality and fraternity but in a relationship of judge to culpable. Apologetic can be carried on only by a person who knows or thinks he knows that truth is a *possession,* and, obviously, that he possesses this possession.

Discussion, on the other hand, is possible only among men who realize that they are englobed by truth and who know that the search for truth never ends in a possessing of it but rather that the ultimate face of truth is always mysterious. Yet this does not mean that discussion must remain spiritless and that the contesting of the other's position cannot take the form of an attack. Discussion would lose its ethical seriousness if it were not a reciprocal calling-into-question.

Not controversy, then, nor apologetic. Rather, our study is meant to be ecumenical, if it is true that ecumenism is the dialogue of churches—and consequently, of theologies —with the end in view of rediscovering unity, a unity that exists in the very foundation of these churches; and if it is true that the method of ecumenism is the reciprocal calling-into-question of the doctrinal affirmations of the churches.

To be sure, it would seem that ecumenical dialogue can be undertaken more easily and more usefully on the level of dogmatic and ecclesiological problems than on the level of ethical problems. Whatever be the depth of the separations that have come between the churches, the style of Christian life has best resisted the division. There has always been a certain consensus regarding ethical values. Although profound disputes have made their appearance, they have appeared on the interior of each church as well as between the churches themselves. (Think, for example, of Pascal and the Jesuits.) This is what has justified the axiom of the first ecumenical generations of our century: "Doctrine divides, action unites." In the face of the ethical doctrines of Nietzsche, of Karl Marx, or of atheism, Christians of every confession quite easily felt their unity. In the face of injustice and misery, a concerted action became possible, and the World Council of Churches and the Roman Catholic Church presently are exploring these possibilities of concerted action. By a paradox, and truly speaking, a rather sad paradox, the churches break the Eucharistic Communion more readily than they break communion in a certain style of ethical life.

Yet we would be wrong in thinking that the realm of action in a Christian perspective can be relatively independent of the realm of faith, that an ethic can be common to churches which do not have the same confession of faith. Where this is the case, is it not in reality that what one calls Christian ethics is nothing more than the ensemble of values common to an age, to a civilization, to a type of society, or in other words, a sort of social consensus more or less colored by Christianity? When Christians too facilely think that they have preserved the same ethic despite doctrinal divisions, and that this ethic is independent of the certitudes of faith, are they not dupes of a sociological illusion?

Of course, this practical consensus which is established

in a society also has its value, and the task of theology is to draw out its significance, just as it is the task of theology to study the conditions of life of a civil society which is religiously divided. But it would be truly to misunderstand the existential reality of the Christian faith to think that it does not call for specific ethical attitudes, that it proposes no light for action other than that of the surrounding society. It would be to forget that faith, while being trust in and adherence to a revelation, is at the same time obedience, and that this obedience is informed by the object of faith. This link between the moral life and faith is drawn out quite clearly by Sec. 23 of Vatican II's decree on ecumenism; when it says that although "in moral matters there are many Christians who do not always understand the gospel in the same way as Catholics, and do not admit the same solutions for the more difficult problems of modern society," nevertheless they, like Catholics, want to adhere to the word of Christ as the source of Christian strength and to follow the precept of the apostle: "Whatever you are doing, whether you speak or act, do everything in the name of the Lord Jesus, giving thanks to God the Father through him" (Col. 3:17, NEB). And the decree goes on to say that it is here that the ecumenical dialogue on the ethical application of the gospel can begin.

This text reminds us that doctrinal divergences have a direct influence on ethical attitudes. One need mention only a problem as concrete as that of birth control to see that such a human and such a banal activity as procreation and the specifically human mode of procreation poses dogmatic questions concerning what constitutes nature and creation, and the limits of human freedom in the midst of this creation. It also reminds us that even on the common axiom of the glorification of the Lord's name in our daily life, divergences are possible and that they are therefore the subject for an ecumenical dialogue.

I would also like to make some remarks on the method that we will follow:

12

1. The difficulty of our subject comes from the fact that Catholic ethics and Protestant ethics are not monolithic realities, and that if we want to institute a true dialogue, we cannot restrict ourselves to the problems as they were posed in the sixteenth century, nor can we contrast a Protestant ethic of today with the ethic of the Counter-Reformation. Theologies are always in flux, and how much more so, ethics. For ethics does not invent its problems: they are presented by the historical situations in which men live. The duty of submission to the state takes completely different aspects according to whether one considers a state whose function is solely military, diplomatic, and internal policing, or whether it is a matter of a democratic state with an economic, social, and cultural vocation. The problem of war in an atomic age takes on a different meaning than it did during the age of muskets. Ethics is always in situation, which does not mean that it is an ethic of situation, that is to say, an ethic which thinks that history alone is normative. Thus we must concentrate our attention on the Protestant and Catholic ethics as they exist or as they seek each other today by reason of the problems that contemporary life forces them to raise.

2. But at the same time, we must keep in mind that these changing ethics, although obliged by history to make perpetual revision, remain part of an ensemble of theological options that become modified much less and sometimes even cannot be modified, because the object concerning which these options have been taken—the revelation of God in Christ—is an immutable object. Consequently, we must go back toward the past, to the epochs in which a basic option was taken. In view of our subject, this epoch for us naturally will be that of the Reformation of the sixteenth century. Thus we shall begin by describing the way in which the ethical problem was defined by the Reformers and their Catholic counterparts, and in what dogmatic context the problem of the Christian life was posed. This will permit us to appreciate better the development that followed.

3. Like the changes of civilization, the confusions of human life created by an industrial society which is also a society of consumption unceasingly call forth new problems. And as collective imperatives penetrate more and more deeply into personal and familial life, we will understand more easily that at present the Christian ethic, whether it be Catholic or Protestant, does not have ready-made answers for all the problems. The Second Vatican Council (in its constitution *Gaudium et Spes*) and the Ecumenical Conference on Church and Society (Geneva, July, 1966) both witness, in their own ways, to a great uncertainty and a great inquietude. One of the characteristics of contemporary Christianity is that if it wants to remain honest, it cannot maintain an unequivocal attitude on all questions in the ethical realm, no matter what be the clarity and firmness of principles. Take a problem such as that of private property, which for a long time was unanimously considered to be regulated either by the law of God or by natural law: today it is such a complex problem that one hesitates to resolve it by a simple formula. Such hesitation is not necessarily the sign of a decline. But it does mean that today the churches are much closer to the *homo viator*, who even when he has a certain and assured faith, is forced, just like the atheist, to move gropingly and with hesitation, and for whom historical becoming has become much more difficult to decipher than for his predecessors. After all, such a situation can serve to remind the churches and their theologians of an ethical virtue that they have always preached or taught, but by applying it to others—the virtue of humility.

I

THE SITUATION OF ETHICS
IN THE THEOLOGY
OF THE REFORMATION
AND IN CATHOLIC THEOLOGY

In the sixteenth century there undoubtedly was a general consensus concerning what man should do. Obedience assuredly was the first of the Christian virtues, obedience to the Word of God or obedience to the ecclesiastical authority—but also obedience to all the established authorities (the fathers, the employers, the magistrates), who were considered as instituted by God, as holders of an incontestable power. No doubt one knew perfectly (and the Reformers better than all the others) that sin also inhabited the hearts of the authorities and that the authorities could be wicked and unjust. But one also knew that evil, thanks to the grace of God, could be turned to man's good, and that one thus had to be patient in regard to the unjust authorities. God would chastise them one day, and in any event, they could not take the Christian from the powerful hand of God.

To be sure, the changes of political regimes, the overthrow of thrones, the conflicts of priesthood and empire introduced a certain inquietude into this stable universe. Was it permitted to kill a tyrant? Was it permitted to revolt? (Think of the problem posed for Luther by the Peasants' Revolt.) But in general, theologians of every confession were agreed in affirming that the right of revolt was circumscribed within very narrow limits. Calvin had dared justify revolt, but he did so with extreme prudence.

15

Human life was seen as unfolding according to the norms of each one's station. Each person had the duties of his station and should not deviate from them. This was one way of applying the apostolic precept: "Let each be content with what he has." The various stations represented a fixed and rigid order, related to the cosmic order. One was born noble or commoner, and each had certain duties belonging to his station. Consequently, each knew what he had to do and there was no discussion about it.

Ethical discussion did not concern the content of ethics. At most, the Reformation had introduced an element of disturbance on one particular point: whereas in the church the religious calling was considered the Christian state par excellence, Luther threw suspicion on such a state. He showed that it was a way of shirking the true duties of one's station—in particular, the duties toward parents. Luther gave renewed value to the secular state by recalling that profession is also a *Beruf*, that is, both profession and vocation at one and the same time. By renouncing his monastic state and by inciting others to follow suit, Luther, on this particular point, introduced a breach into the idea of an immobile and stable social universe. But the breach was slight and carefully repaired.

Although there was little discussion on the content of ethics, there was discussion on the meaning of ethics. What was posed was the whole problem of the meaning and import of works in relation to salvation. The Catholic Church had never formally taught the heretical doctrine of salvation by man's good works, and certain of its doctors had to resort to a kind of Pelagianism or semi-Pelagianism in order to make precise the respective parts played by God's grace and man's will in the realization of salvation. Yet, on the level of practice—of a practice duly authorized and encouraged by the hierarchy—the church made good works an instrument, if not the principal instrument, of salvation. Of course, the development of the doctrine of merit and of satisfactory works had made the theological terrain

16

more unstable and had prepared consciences for a *de facto* Pelagianism. But, in fact, it was really religious practice which prepared the way for this debasement. In a sermon preached at Erfurt on October 21, 1522, Luther emphasized that the danger resided not in an officially proclaimed doctrine, but in a faith. "Thus I am concerned," he said, "because in our day there are so many of these false saints who rely upon their works, and who deceive themselves and others with good works (as they call them). They say, it is true, 'Our works are nothing,' and yet they call free will into play. But what grace is and what faith is, they know less than a goose knows the Psalter. So be on guard against a fabricated and contrived faith." [1]

Thus the whole effort of the Reformation bore both upon a restoration of the doctrine of justification and on returning works to their proper place. Faith is false if it is not followed by works. But works are born from faith as spontaneously as the good tree bears good fruit. The Formula of Concord summarizes as follows the points that were undisputed among the theologians of the Confession of Augsburg: "God wants the faithful to practice good works, such is his order and commandment; truly good works are neither those which one conceives for oneself, with good intentions, nor those which one does in order to conform to human prescriptions, but those which God himself has prescribed in his Word: they are not the effect of our own natural forces, and they do not come about until the person has been reconciled with God through faith and renewed by the Holy Spirit, or as the apostle Paul says, 'created in Christ Jesus to devote ourselves to . . . good deeds' (Eph. 2:10, NEB)." [2] In fact, the Confession of Augsburg had already detailed the place of works in relation to faith and the *necessity* of works that were *not necessary* for salvation: "We teach that it is absolutely necessary to do good works not in order to place one's trust in them and in order to merit grace, but for the love of God

17

and for his glory. It is always faith alone that grasps grace and the remission of sins. Since the Holy Spirit is given (to us) through faith, the heart thus becomes capable of accomplishing good works. For before, not having the Holy Spirit, it is too feeble" (Art. XX).

The same doctrine, which is a consequence of that of justification, is found again and again in the symbolic writings of the Reformation. For example, the Confession of La Rochelle declares, in Art. XXII: "Thus faith not only does not dampen the desire to live a good and holy life, but engenders and quickens it within us, necessarily producing good works. Moreover, although God regenerates us, in order to bring about our salvation, reforming us to do good, nevertheless we confess that the good works which we do by the guidance of the Holy Spirit do not at all count to justify us or to merit our being taken by God as his children. For we would always be wavering in doubt and inquietude if our consciences did not rely on the satisfaction by which Christ has set us free."

This unanimous doctrine, whatever be the certainty of its Scriptural basis, is nevertheless a difficult doctrine. The difficulty concerns the necessity of works. With Paul as well as James, the Reformation held that a faith of sluggish nature, one which would not produce in us the fruits of love, hope, and patience, would be a suspect faith, a faith that would destroy one within, a dead faith. Works (that is, sanctification and the ethical life, for the Reformation refused to define isolated good works set in a juridical framework) —works so understood are an internal necessity of faith. But they are not necessary for salvation, for reconciliation with God, for the forgiveness of sins. Their necessity is relative not to the accession to pardon and to grace, but to the life of faith and in faith. Consequently, the Reformation had to sustain a double thesis, to formulate its doctrine in a dialectical fashion, to say both yes and no to the necessity of works.

But this general doctrine of the Reformation does not
18

exhaust all the aspects of the ethical life that were emphasized by the various Reformers.

1. *The Bases and Meaning of Ethics According to Luther*

For Luther, of course, ethics found its basis in justification. The latter determines ethics in the sense that it is the presupposition of ethics (*Vorzeichen,* according to the expression of Paul Althaus) [3] and the source of ethics. The term "source" should be taken in a concrete way: the ethical life flows from justification, to the point that the category of duty and obligation ceases to be basic and the whole ethical life is lived under the sign of spontaneity: *"Fatemur opera bona fidem sequi debere, imo non debere, sed sponte sequi, sicut arbor bona non debet bonos fructus facere, sed sponte facit."* [4] This was why Luther was reticent to speak of the third use of the law. He was afraid of destroying ethical spontaneity, of putting man once again under the constraint of the law. This is why he wanted to make it only a benevolent guide. Moreover, not only can sinful man not obtain salvation through his works, since the latter are not good (there is a spontaneity in sin as well as in righteousness), but even if man were capable of righteousness, he could not attain salvation through this righteousness, for it is contrary to the divinity of God for salvation to be other than a free act of divine grace. Thus the action of man cannot have salvation as its finality. It can have no other meaning than gratitude for salvation previously given by God. This theme of gratitude as the motivation and finality of the ethical life was given an important place by the Heidelberg Catechism. Consequently, it is maintained that this theme is characteristic of Reformed thought. But it is equally at the heart of Luther's thought. For Luther, however, the moral act has another teleological meaning. It is entirely oriented toward the

19

neighbor. No longer is it a matter of satisfying God, but of serving the neighbor. In the sermon of Erfurt referred to previously, Luther declares: "This faith is awakened in us by God. From this come also works, by which we come to the aid of our neighbor and serve him."

Good and evil have no existence in and of themselves: an act becomes good to the extent that it is received by the grace of God. To receive man into his mercy means for God at the same time to receive man's acts and to justify them—which implies an essential unity of man and his acts. Pushing to the end of his theological logic, Luther considered that an act conforming to the commandment of God would not yet be good, in the sense that Althaus calls "metaethical": to be sure, the act must conform to the commandment of God, but it must also be offered to the justification of God. In other words, the ethically good act—good because it conforms to the commandment—nevertheless has no value in God's eyes, if it is not in the faith of justification when it is accomplished. Conversely, despite its impurity, an act can be good when it is accomplished in the faith that God has already saved us in advance. This enabled Luther to assert, in what is certainly an equivocal formula, that faith is the good work par excellence, since by it goodness is conferred to all other works. Thus there would be no question that the works of pagans can be good in the ethical sense and that they are socially useful. But this ethical stage is not decisive for judging the goodness of a work. Thus, for Luther, things never have their own nature; they are what they are by the grace of God who receives them and gives them a future.

Since the Christian is no longer tied to the ethical categories and to their absoluteness, nor to the absoluteness of the hierarchies of value, he will be available for every act which the situation—that is, the neighbor—calls for. Thus the Christian differs absolutely from the person who seeks to obtain his salvation through works and who therefore searches for acts that are out of the ordinary, who will try to add supererogatory acts to what the law of God requires of all, who will follow not only the "precepts" but the "evangelical counsels" as well.

This freedom in regard to the exploits of "holiness" and this teleological orientation of action toward the neighbor resulted in Luther's rehabilitation of secular life and action. One's gratitude to God is better witnessed to in the honest and banal exercise of a profession that is useful to the neighbor than in the affectations of asceticism. One reason why Luther was so hostile to the monastic life was precisely that he saw in monasticism the double temptation of wanting the extraordinary (whereas the most profane action is holy when it is done in faith in justification) and of turning aside from the neighbor. As Max Weber has seen quite well, even though Luther evidenced much less comprehension and interest than Calvin for the modern forms of life and of economic expansion, he nonetheless gave impetus to the modern human adventure by his rehabilitation of the secular.

When man moved solely in ethical categories, when he knew God only through his law, he did not have knowledge of the authentic essence of God. Only the act of justification puts man in the presence of the true God and God then gives himself to man in a communion in love. When man knew only the accusing and impossible law of God, he could only hate this law which condemned him. Now that Christ, who has fulfilled this law, inhabits the heart of man through the Holy Spirit and puts a man's heart on the proper course of a spontaneous fulfillment of the law, the law has become precious in man's eyes.

Thus what characterizes Luther's ethics is the abandonment of any absolutistic pretensions (specifically, the pretension of being able to define a good in itself, which because it is related to the commandment of God would be a means of approaching God) : one must lose one's ethic if one wishes to find it, and when one has rediscovered it, it has a very humble finality. No longer is it designed to please God—only faith makes God rejoice—now ethics is designed to serve men and to build up the human community here below.

2. The Bases and Meaning of Ethics
    According to Calvin

One frequently finds Luther and Calvin being put into opposition on the level of ethics. The sternness credited rightly or wrongly to Calvin; his insistence on the law, in its third use; his constant recourse to the Old Testament to clarify moral questions; the fact that he put the Old Testament on exactly the same level as the New Testament; the fact also that later Calvinism has very often added ecclesiastical discipline to the two marks of the church—all these facts join together to present Calvinist ethics as tainted with a secret legalism. We will show, however, that such is not the case, and that although Calvinist ethics and Lutheran ethics have a different style, they nonetheless follow identical theological routes.

There is no doubt that Calvin attached a decisive importance to ethics. An important appendix, *On the Christian Life,* was added to the 1539 edition of the *Institutes of the Christian Religion,* and this text was then integrated into the body of the work and developed in five chapters at the time of the last edition. In 1550, Calvin even made a separate edition of this ethical part of the *Institutes.*

But the basis of ethics for Calvin was the same that we have already stated for Luther.[5] The ethical life does not consist of good works which would acquire merit for us and assure our salvation. That which Calvin indistinctly calls "regeneration" or "sanctification" proceeds only from our insertion in Christ by faith. The moral life is the manifestation of Christ's inhabiting in us through his Spirit. Calvin calls it sanctification in order to mark its continuous nature, for the holiness of the believer was never ac-

22

quired once for all. He calls it regeneration because he saw in it the reestablishment of the image of God: "Because this image has been effaced by sin, it must now be restored in Christ . . . the regeneration of believers is nothing other than a reformation of the image of God in them." [6] The restoration of this image, which is the very content of our ethical life, is part of the work of God and comes from the secret operation of the Holy Spirit. This operation of the Holy Spirit produces in us both a mortification of the old man and a participation in the new life. These two aspects are not successive moments, but are always joined, as the cross and the resurrection are always found together.[7]

The new man quickened by the Holy Spirit has no existence in and of itself. It exists only in Christ and cohabits with an old man who, although mortified, is not dead. The idea of *semper justus ac peccator,* although the formula was not taken up by Calvin, is immanent in his thought. "We continue to be sinners, while being progressively sanctified." [8] This is why the Christian life presents itself as a constant battle. "This restoration (of the image of God) is completed neither in a moment of time, nor in a day, nor in a year: but God abolishes the corruptions of the flesh in his elect through a continual succession of time, and even bit by bit; and does not cease to purge them of their filth, to consecrate them as temples, to reform their understanding to a true purity, in order for them to live all their life in penitence and to know that this conflict will end only at death." [9] This text is remarkable in the sense that its central affirmation is that God, who brings about sanctification within us, in no way destroys our existence as ethical subject engaged in the conflict. "By regeneration the children of God are delivered from the bondage of sin, but not as if they had already obtained full possession of freedom, and no longer felt any annoyance from the flesh. Materials for an unremitting contest remain, that they may be exercised, and not only exercised, but may better understand their weakness." [10] The structure of this phrase is identical with the first: it begins with God as the subject and ends with a proposition of which man is the subject. This structure is characteristic of Calvin's thought: God works in order that we may act. To wage "open war without end and unceasingly" [11]—such is the ethical condition of the man regenerated by the grace of God. Certainly one finds this same accent in Luther's thought, but there it is dominated by another note, that of ethical spontaneity. And this difference explains why the place given to law is more considerable in Calvin than in Luther: it is a weapon for combat and we have need of its spur. "But although the law comprehends within it that new life by which the image of God is restored in us, yet, as our sluggishness stands greatly in need both of helps and incentives, it will be useful to collect out of Scripture a true account of this reformation, lest any who have a heartfelt desire of repentance should in their zeal go astray." [12]

Election is the foundation of new life, the condition *sine qua non* of ethical existence. But at the same time, this ethical life constitutes the finality of election. We are elected by God in order to lead a holy life. The certitude of election will lead the faithful "to renounce himself, to carry his cross, and to orient his whole attitude towards the future life." [13] As Calvin writes in the *Institutes,* "God reigns when men, in denial of themselves, and contempt of this world and this earthly life, devote themselves to righteousness and aspire to heaven." [14] Calvin's insistence on this theme of renunciation is very strong. The same theme is also found in Luther, but, as Wendel emphasizes,[15] in Luther renunciation and penitence must open the way to a knowledge of Christ; they constitute a preaching of previous repentance and are attached to the second use of the law. In 1536, Calvin had adopted this point of view. However, he consciously turned away from it, and from 1539 on, he reversed the order of the terms. It is only by faith in Christ that man is led to a discovery of his sin, to repentance, to mortification, and to renunciation. Naturally, this renunciation is not extended in its exclusively ascetic and negative sense. On the contrary, it is a matter of manifesting this renunciation in assistance to the neighbor. But the duties of charity "are not fulfilled by the mere discharge of them, though none be omitted, unless it is done from a pure feeling of love." [16] This quite positive note coincides with that which we have already noted in Luther. It does not hinder Calvin, however, from coming back unceasingly to the nature of the pain, conflict, and suffering that the life of the justified and pardoned Christian represents. "Those whom the Lord has chosen and honoured with his intercourse must prepare for a hard, laborious, troubled life, a life full of many and various kinds of evils: it being the will of our heavenly Father to exercise his people in this way while putting them to the proof. Having begun this course with Christ the first-born, he continues it towards all his children. For though that Son was dear to him . . . yet we see, that far from being treated gently and indulgently, we may say, that not only was he subjected to a perpetual cross while he dwelt on earth, but his whole life was nothing else than a kind of perpetual cross. . . . Hence it affords us great consolation in hard and difficult circumstances, which men deem evil and adverse, to think that we are holding fellowship with the sufferings of Christ; that as he passed to celestial glory through a labyrinth of many woes, so we too are conducted thither through various tribulations . . . the more we are afflicted with adversity, the surer we are made of our fellowship with Christ." [17] Running through this passage, and many similar passages, is the theme of the imitation of Christ. The theme of the imitation of Christ is set in a doctrine of election: it is not by dint of imitation that we arrive at Christ and grace; it is because we already are incorporated in him by a free decision of divine grace that we have the possibility of imitating him. And this imitation seals our communion with him.

It certainly is tempting to see in this doctrine of Calvin

25

the reflection of his experience and of the experience of all the faithful of his day, who because of their faith were exposed to the sufferings of persecution and martyrdom. But without denying in the least that Calvin's vision was colored by a historical experience, it is necessary to recognize that in fact this attitude is commanded by the structure of his theology.

It can appear paradoxical that this ethic, which gives such a prominent place to the ideas of conflict, suffering, renunciation, mortification, and scorn for the world in the expectation of eternal life, in no way resulted, as did so many medieval ethics utilizing the same themes, in a condemnation of profane existence. On the contrary, in a much stronger way than that of Luther, Calvin's ethic oriented minds toward concrete realizations, toward the building of a completely new economy and society. André Bieler has recently written a small book titled *Calvin, prophète de l'ère industrielle* [18] ("Calvin, Prophet of the Industrial Era"), in which he has characterized the Calvinist ethic both as an ethic that is strictly Christological—which it indeed is—and as a "Biblical ethic in tune with the dynamism of history."

To be sure, Luther also rehabilitated secular work. But in conformity to the medieval perspective, he enclosed secular work in the stable and definitive "states" of an immobile society. Calvin, on the other hand, who on this point was much more turned toward the future than the past, was able to perceive the economic transformations that were coming and the expansion that was being prepared. And he wanted to arm the faithful for the battle. This was the source of his extremely audacious attitude regarding the question of interest-bearing loans, which was decisive for the future of commercial and industrial capitalism. He did not feel himself bound by the Old Testament's condemnation of usury, since, in his view, there was a basic difference between sustenance borrowing and productive borrowing. He even saw that the law given to Israel was

26

conditioned by the situation of that people and that we cannot simply transpose it to different sociological conditions. Speaking of the particular legislation given to Israel, Calvin wrote: "The Lord did not deliver it by the hand of Moses to be promulgated in all countries, and to be everywhere enforced; but having taken the Jewish nation under his special care, patronage, and guardianship, he was pleased to be specially its legislator, and as became a wise legislator, he had special regard to it in enacting laws." [19]

Is the paradox deep-rooted or only apparent? Certainly one can say that two ethics are reflected in Calvin, one marked by the Scholastic tradition and oriented toward renunciation, the other a newer one, oriented toward the work of civilization, toward the future, toward accomplishments for the glory of God, toward the insertion of human work in a world that is and must be "the theater of God's glory." But these two orientations are not simply juxtaposed: in any event, man will have to fight and to suffer; if he has a work to accomplish, it is not to receive glory from it, it is not for personal satisfaction. It is to fulfill "the duties of charity." We can say that the Calvinist ethic has turned out generations of enterprising, active, and successful men, but not in a hedonistic or eudaemonistic perspective. The work of sanctification is carried on through the renunciations that creation and expansion require.

3. Traditional Catholic Ethics

Although today Catholic ethics is in the process of full development and profound transformation, the Catholic Church lived through many centuries with a stable ethics. It is important for us to grasp the spirit of this ethics. This traditional ethics has two sources which are not necessarily oriented in the same direction: the Thomistic ethics, which constitutes its backdrop, and the practical modifications that came unexpectedly during the course of the nineteenth century.

First, let us consider the principles of Thomist ethics. Saint Thomas attached a great importance to ethics. The *Secunda* of the *Summa* is devoted to this subject. His system consists in a Christianization of Aristotelian ethics, in which all of ethics resides in the movement of the rational creature toward God. The goal of this movement is salvation, which constitutes the final end of the rational creature and this final end is the intuitive vision of God. Thus ethics is this ascending movement of the rational creature toward the Creator, and the contemplation of the Creator constitutes the equivalent of what the ethical systems of antiquity called the *Highest Good*. Being a question of arriving at supreme knowledge, the intellect would play a central role.

The means that lead to this end are the moral works of man. The intelligence is aided and sustained by the will and especially by freedom. But it is not a pure will that is involved. "The free will is rooted in reason, which proposes to the will the objects of its efforts and the motives of its action." [20]

Now, the idea of the good irresistibly attracts the will. The good (like the Ideas of Platonic thought) exercises a sort of attraction over it. This happens in such a way that freedom does not consist in the possibility of doing no matter what; rather, it is directed to the good as its ultimate end. It is only in regard to the multiplicity of goods that free will can exercise its power of choice. Since the ultimate end is being, an action is good insofar as it participates in being, insofar as it has within it a perfection that conforms it to being. Moral evil is only a quantitative absence of being and perfection, that is to say, Saint Thomas did not recognize the positive reality of sin.

Besides the reason and the will, feeling also plays a role in the moral life, but it is a secondary role. Emotions and passions play a role as stimulus of moral aspirations.

Moral acts are governed by principles, some of which are internal and some of which are external. The internal principles are the virtues, natural or supernatural, which sustain the soul in its movement toward the final end. In accordance with Aristotle's thought, there is a relationship between virtue and habitus: virtue is a good habitus, whose stability guarantees man's moral life. Sin comes into the picture here and only here; it is not at the heart of the definition of ethics, but only of the obstacles. Sin is nothing other than a bad habitus, that is to say, not adapted to the end of the reasonable man. Among all the virtues (the three theological virtues and the four cardinal virtues), the supernatural charity or love for God and neighbor obviously plays a central role. The fact that it is a habitus like all the virtues manifestly weakens the nature of love as supernatural gift.

The external principle of morality is God himself acting on man through his law and his grace. By his law, to quote Grabmann, God "gives us the norm, the rule, the content and the sanction of morality" (Saint Thomas I, II, 90–108).[21] By his grace, he sustains us and raises us: the law of God essentially is the *lex aeterna,* from which are derived all the particular laws. It has a cosmic import, that is to say, it is applied to all the creatures, rational and nonrational. However, whereas the nonrational creatures are mechanistically subdued by it, man alone is capable by his reason of knowing the end of this law and of adhering to it by his will, so that the acts which he carries out are those of a free and conscious subject.

This *lex aeterna,* accessible to reason, merits being called natural law. It is inscribed in human nature and is recognized by man when he awakens to reason. The positive revelation of the Old and New Testaments aids in confirming this natural law, but at the same time revelation assigns supernatural ends to man. It is the language that God uses to address himself to that in man which has a supernatural destiny.

29

God also is the dispenser of supernatural grace, and this grace sustains man in the fulfillment of his supernatural destiny. As dispenser of grace, God "is the driving, cooperating, and elevating principle which, coming from outside, grasps the human soul down to its depths. God fills the soul with a supernatural system of forces which confer a divine form on the soul's being and action, and brings it into intimate harmony with the most elevated end, with the intuitive vision of God." [22]

Thus the ethics of Saint Thomas, which naturally extends to a minute examination of all particular acts and readily turns morality into psychology, claims to unite the immanent and the transcendent, the objective and the subjective, in a synthesis. On the one hand, moral action flows forth from within man. It expresses the spirituality and the freedom of man. On the other hand, it is determined by objective and external norms, and receives its orientation from a supreme end that acts upon freedom without contradicting it. For this freedom is that of a rational being who, insofar as he has been created such, is normally ordained to this supreme end. Grace is added to man's nature from without, in order to lead him without violence to his end—so true it is that grace fulfills nature without destroying it. This is why Saint Thomas set himself to showing "the points where the supernatural is linked to the natural," [23] and to showing also that the needs of the natural soul are filled by the graces of the supernatural order.

As Grabmann emphasizes, there is a profound tie between morality and salvation, since the intuitive vision of God constitutes salvation and since salvation is the proper end of morality. One can understand that this leaves the field open for a doctrine of salvation by works, although Saint Thomas never taught such a doctrine. The hope of salvation that ultimately crowns our moral life constitutes, by a kind of resurgence of ancient eudaemonism, the most powerful motive for the moral life, and consequently the

Christian soul is led to perform moral works with a view to the beatitude of salvation.

Grace is far from being absent in this system, but instead of human freedom being the response to divine grace, this freedom itself is preexistent and only receives the aid of grace. The ensemble of the system is more theocentric than Christocentric, not because it does not concern the Trinitarian God and because grace is separated from Christ, but because Thomist ethics does not take its departure in the new life into which man enters by justification. It is rooted in an anthropology in which man is by nature ordained to being.

The second source of the traditional ethics of the Catholic Church is not a theological system, but a practical reformation that has continuously brought significant consequences over the course of the centuries. The following passages from a work by Father Pinckaers illustrate this: "The Council of Trent, preoccupied with the education of priests, decided on the creation of seminaries, in which theological education geared to the pastoral ministry would be dispensed. One could not impose upon the priests the task of following the theological courses given in the universities, nor even of taking the treatises studied in these faculties as the basis of instruction. Such courses were for the most part too long and too difficult; they were too much concerned with abstract and speculative questions; without much concern for the concrete problems which the priests would encounter in their parish ministries, in spiritual counseling, and in the administration of the sacrament of penance. Thus it was necessary to create a new type of manual of theology, one adapted to the needs of the seminaries and to the pastoral concerns of parish priest.

"The Jesuit Juan Azor composed the first modern-type manual of moral theology, around sixteen hundred. The work was titled *Institutes morales*. There he expounded moral theology according to the following purpose: to establish briefly the fundamental principles of this science, then in the light of these principles to examine all practical problems (or 'cases of conscience' as they were then called) that priests might face, especially in the ministry of the confessional. In an important innovation, Father Azor arranged the moral material according to the order of the commandments of God, of the church, and finally, of the seven sacraments. This new formula met with great success, and during this period there was a general distribution of ethics manuals devoted to the study of cases of conscience, of all possible cases, and even sometimes of imaginary cases. In his work *Resolutiones morales,* the Sicilian Theatine Diana collected some twenty thousand cases. This was the origin of casuistry." [24]

Father Pinckaers then characterizes this new moral orientation in the following fashion:

a. First of all, it takes up certain elements of Thomistic thought and schematizes them: it grounds moral acts in *freedom;* their good or bad character is estimated in relation to the *law.* This law is expressed in commandments and is imposed on freedom by the intermediary of the conscience. Law imposed the tie of obligation on freedom. Consequently, moral theory would develop in an essentially juridical framework, a framework that is imposed by what was called "the tribunal of penitence." "We see there a judge, the conscience, charged with the function of applying the law and of punishing infractions; in the face of conscience and the law, we find the subject of the law, the contingent accused: freedom, the one responsible for the acts of men." [25] Thus this moral system would develop within a framework more and more legalistic and would resurrect Pharisaism. Like the latter, it would ask only two questions: What is it that one may do; What is it that one may not do? We are diametrically opposed to the Pauline ethics: "Christ set us free, to be free men" (Gal. 5:1, NEB).

b. Like all Pharisaism, this morality would tend toward

32

minimalism: "The theology whose object is to make legal obligations more precise will attach itself above all to the determination of the minimum required in order to be in line with the law, that which one can and must require of all." [26]

c. As in all legalism, the dread of sin would be dominant and one would attempt to establish precisely the shape of sin, the types of sin, their degree of gravity—which, in relation to Thomist ethics, oriented toward the intuitive and blessed vision of God, constitutes a sort of decadence.

It is worthwhile to reflect on the meaning of this development. It represents the triumph of pedagogy over ethics. Beginning with the time when ethical problems are viewed under the angle of pedagogy, the legalism inherent in all pedagogy becomes insidious. Moreover, this pedagogy is a very special pedagogy; it is that of the sacrament of penance. Now, the theology implicit in this sacrament is eminently suspect; it signifies that acts of men designed to atone for or efface fault are substituted for the free grace of God who pardons, who creates a new life in man through justification. The sacrament of penance is designed to render us worthy of receiving the Eucharistic Sacrament. The penitential practice which has played a primary role in Catholicism has thus thrown ethics toward a legalism and a legalism that claims to bring God a satisfaction.

These two sources of Catholic ethics have gone along hand in hand, but penitential morality has largely overshadowed the Thomist contribution. What image can one draw of Catholic moral theory as it has been practiced and taught up until very recent date? It is easy to obtain this image by referring to the article on "Moral Theory" in the *Dictionnaire de théologie catholique*.[27] To be sure, all contemporary theologians would state that this work is outdated on almost all subjects. That is true. But it remains nonetheless that this work, being marked by no extreme tendencies and seeking a middle-of-the-road point of view, has represented a sort of broad consensus, and it is for this reason that we refer to it.

The Thomist inspiration appears from the very definition of Christian ethics: "Moral theology is that part of theology which, in the light of revealed principles, treats of human acts from the point of view of their direction toward ultimate supernatural ends, or, according to the definition that one can deduce from Saint Thomas, it is the part of theology that treats of human acts, *'Secundum quod per eos ordinatur homo ad perfectam Dei contemplationem, in qua aeterna beatitudo constitit'* " (*Summa theol.* I^a, q. I, ad. 4).

Or again, it has as its object "the study of human acts considered according to their relationship of propriety or impropriety with the ultimate supernatural end willed by God as obligatory for all men, whether in their individual lives or in their social life." [28]

It follows from these definitions that ethics is not at all conceived independently from revelation, but that revelation is reduced to a certain number of principles, that the moral life has the goal of man's salvation, and that this salvation consists, as in the Greek philosophies, in the blessed contemplation of God. Ethics is presented as the way that leads to the knowledge of God. Thus it can be defined independently of the work of justification accomplished by God in Christ.

This impression is confirmed again when one examines the content of ethics: this content is basically and exclusively the law: "The divine rule, according to which human acts must be guided, is primarily and principally the eternal law defined by Saint Thomas, *'Ratio divinae sapientiae secundum quod est directiva omnium actum et notionum'* (*Summa theol.* I^a, II^{ae}, q. XCIII, a. 1). From it flow all the moral obligations imposed on man, by divine natural law, by divine positive or supernatural law, and by the double human law, ecclesiastical and civil, emanating from divine law and conformed to its direction."

The task of moral theology seems primarily to be that

of defining these different laws which should orient human action. "The divine natural law, defined by Saint Thomas (I^a, II^{ae}, q. XCI, a. 2), 'Participatio legis aeternae in rationali creatura,' imposes on man duties coming from nature itself vis-à-vis God, vis-à-vis himself and his fellowmen.

"The divine positive or supernatural law, in the present order of Providence, has as its object the supernatural means by which the end must be obtained. They amount to two principal categories. The first category is that of the supernatural virtues, by which man, under the direction of the church, is enabled to know the supernatural end and to direct all his affections toward it in order to obtain it effectively. The second category is that of the Sacraments, which were established by Our Lord and entrusted to his Church in order to give, maintain, or restore the supernatural life of grace." [29]

All obligations certainly have their ultimate source in God, even the obligations that proceed from our nature. But it should be noticed that all these obligations are forces of authority which are exercised over man to constrain him to realize both his nature and his supernature. Nowhere is it a question of freedom. Freedom undoubtedly is required on the level of each individual act, but it does not define the substance of the ethical life.

This impression of legalism is again reinforced when one considers the double human law, the ecclesiastical and the civil:

a. Ecclesiastical law: "In consequence of the divine providential command confiding to the church the direction of all the faithful in the use of the means of salvation, the *ecclesiastical law* determines, for the utility of all the faithful, what they must fulfill in order to lead more securely to their supernatural end." The meaning of ethics appears quite clearly here: God has established an objective order of salvation in the world. Man is placed in this order, as man according to Plato is placed in the eternal order of the cosmos, and man must conform to it in order to come to his goal. The church to whom this order is confided must then guide man in order for him to arrive at this goal with more security, which means that God isn't absolutely tied to this order. God can save whom he chooses and by the means that he chooses. But it would be risky to rely on this pure grace. It is much better to follow the way of security marked out by the church.

b. Civil law: "In consequence of the divine command establishing man in society and putting him under the dependence of the authority necessary to regulate this society, the *civil law* determines what citizens must accomplish in order to lead to the proper temporal end of this society, without prejudice of the necessary orientation toward the supernatural end (Saint Thomas, *De regimine principum* I, I. C 1. XIV, XV).

"For all that they proceed from a legitimate authority, coming from God, and for all that they are just, civil laws are like emanations of the eternal law, from which they take all of their moral value (Saint Thomas, I^a, II^{ac}, q. XCIII, a. 3; q. XCVI, a. 4)." [30]

Thus all laws form a hierarchical ensemble, within which there is indeed a sort of gradation: all laws do not have the same authority.[31] Yet all are necessary on their own level. Their exact observation procures the assurance of salvation. One will seek in vain for the place of faith in this system. Undoubtedly it is not totally absent. Certain means of salvation, like the sacraments, require it, and in any case, faith comes to sustain man in the fulfillment of his duties. But there is no organic tie between ethics and faith. The effaced role of faith, which is not the foundation of the moral life but only its adjuvant, explains also the absence of freedom.

To be sure, this freedom is partially recuperated in a domain that indeed belongs to the moral life and that is not, however, under the empire of the law: "Other than the preceptive direction issuing from all these laws, there

36

is also a direction for human acts that is *simply permissive,* declaring what is not the object of any divine or human interdiction, or what is praised and recommended either by divine authority or by ecclesiastical authority. As examples of direction, praising and recommending certain acts as more excellent and more agreeable to God or counselled by the Church, one can mention all the directions connected with the evangelical counsels." [32]

This view is constant in Catholic moral theory and the theologians do their best to preserve it. Catholic secular tradition has always distinguished between the law of God such as it has been promulgated by Jesus Christ and the precepts and counsels. Father Paul de Vooght writes: "Christ did not prescribe but counseled the renunciation of property and of marriage. Thus ecclesiastical authority is not permitted to make an obligation of celibacy or of marriage, of private property or of life in common." [33] One can clearly see that the concern of this theologian is to preserve, by means of this distinction, a margin of freedom for each Christian in regard to ecclesiastical authority.

Thus he shows that according to Saint Thomas obedience toward superiors should not be considered in an absolute fashion. Saint Thomas, in effect, distinguishes three types of obedience: "One, sufficient for salvation, which is obedient in all that is obligatory; another, perfect, which is obedient in all that is lawful; a third, indiscreet, which submits in what is forbidden" (*Summa theol.,* q. 104, art. 5 ad 3). Saint Thomas thus accords an important place to the *mensura rationis* in the discrimination among human orders coming from higher authorities: the *mensura rationis* as moral criterion, the theory of middle acts and neutral acts, and valorization of circumstances as elements allowing the valuation of morality are essential elements of his ethic. The same is true for Saint Bernard, for whom obedience to men does not enter into account where it is a question of absolute good or evil. In both cases the duty of obedience to God is evident. "Between these two extremes (to do an absolutely good act or to reject an integrally bad act), there are intermediate positions in which the morality of the act depends on circumstances of mode, place, time, and person. It is in cases of this type that obedience is imposed, as for example in the case of the tree of the knowledge of good and evil which was in Eden. In such cases, it is not fitting that we impose our opinions on those of the teachers. In these cases, the prescriptions and interdictions of the prelates absolutely cannot be scorned" (D.E.c. XIX, Thom., p. 174).

For Saint Thomas, "no man is ever subject to another man as far as the inner movement of his will is concerned" (*Summa theol.* II^a, II^{ae}, q. 104, art. 5, inc.). Thus obedience is essentially a civic or social virtue that concerns the external form of acts, not their voluntary motivation. Moreover, "all that belongs to the nature of the body" is excluded from this submission. In that, men are to obey only God alone, for "in their nature all men are equal."

In that which concerns the maintenance of the life of the body and of the procreation of descendants, man cannot be forced to obedience. The inferior should obey his superior only in those matters in which he is his superior (*"secundum rationem superioritatis"*) and only in what concerns the regulation of his acts in the framework of the social life (*"ad dispositionem actuum et rerum humanorum"*).

Finally, Saint Thomas does not mean that the value of an act is viewed in the absolute; its perfection does not reside entirely in its conformity to its nature. One must also take account of proper circumstances (*"debitae circonstanciae"*) which respond to the questions: *quis, quod, ubi, quibus auxiliis, cur, quomodo, quando* (*Summa theol.* I^a, II^{ae}, q. 7, art. 3). The *mensura rationis* that judges circumstances is reason subjected to the divine law.[34]

Whether it be a question of the distinction between commands and counsels, of the limits of submission to the authorities, of the domains where the authority of superiors cannot and should not be exercised, of the appreciation of the modalities of an act, in all of these areas we see the effort of Catholic theology to assure a place for freedom in the ethical domain, to guarantee this freedom against the threat of legalism and against the concomitant threat of either ecclesiastical or civil authority (the life of man in the church and in society is always conceived of as unfolding within a hierarchical framework). But this recuperated freedom is not the freedom of faith: it is the freedom conferred by the *mensura rationis*. Reason, enlightened by faith and by ecclesiastical tradition, must maintain a place for freedom in all domains where man does not find himself in the presence of an absolute law or of an authority that expresses itself validly in its own proper domain. The ethics leaves a more or less large place for freedom, but it is not conceived of as an ethic of freedom. Freedom is reinserted into the cracks of the system every time that the restraints of theological and socio-ecclesiastical legalism can be slackened without damage.

This common doctrine, the fruit of Thomism and of the penitential reformation of the seventeenth century, has a very clear incidence on the popular pedagogy of the church. To see this, one need only look at the *Catechism for the Use of the Dioceses of France,*[35] where we find the following picture of ethics: "Ethics is the ensemble of the duties that God imposes upon us"—"There can be no true ethics without God, because God alone can impose duties on all men and reward or punish each one according to his merit"—"Conscience is our reason when it tells us: This must be done because it is good, that must be avoided because it is bad"—"In sum, we find Christian ethics in the commandments of God and of the church."

As far as these commandments are concerned, the Catechism states: "We are obligated to observe the commandments of the church, for Jesus Christ has declared that to disobey the church is to disobey him." Note that these commandments of the church concern: the sanctification

39

of feasts, Sunday Mass, obligatory confession, Easter attend-
ance, fasts during Ember days and Lent, abstaining from
meat on Fridays. It is not difficult to see what theological
asseverations underlie this teaching: (1) the basic characteristic of the Christian life is to be submissive to God's law
and consequently to the authority that represents God;
(2) Since God is the source of ethics, it is universal, which
presupposes that natural law and revealed law are com-
plementary; (3) God is essentially the judge who rewards
men according to their merits; (4) Reason, as the receptacle of the universal law, is the motive force of the moral
life; (5) Christ does not take part in the foundation of the
moral life. He intervenes only to guarantee the commandments of the church and to confer on them an absoluteness
that they would have only with difficulty by themselves.

In a general way, one can say that this common moral
system is lacking the two fundamental dimensions of every
Christian ethic: firstly, the personal relationship of the believer with God, which is completely different from the
purely juridical relationship between a law and an obedient subject, and secondly, the interpersonal relationship.
But these two dimensions introduce risk into the moral
life. For every encounter with God and with the neighbor
brings with it a sort of endogenous insecurity. We know
not where we will be led. Ethical legalism, on the contrary,
is assuring and it develops casuistically in order to increase
this security.[36]

Father Marc Oraison has reacted violently to this traditional Catholic moral teaching, to this ethics which is defined outside of Biblical revelation, which is fixed in place
even before God has spoken. Oraison mercilessly psycho-
analyzes this ethic.[37] He quotes abundantly and indignantly
from a manual of theology currently in use in the seminaries, and although he does not name the author, it is not
difficult to identify him (the work in question is *Katho-
lische Moraltheologie,* by H. Jone). In this work, morality
is easily defined: "Man must attain his ultimate end

40

through personal activity, in conformity with the remote or objective rule and with the near or subjective rule of moral action: the law and the conscience. These rules are violated by sin, their observation is facilitated by the virtues." [38] That is all: all morality thus takes place within an abstract reality, the law and the conscience, a sort of subjective reflection of the law. "It is at least surprising," notes Oraison, "to see Christian ethics defined without the least reference to God known as acting person, and without his even being named. Human activity unfolds and must come to its end independently of the action of God, of which there is no mention. Thus we are advised, from the very first page, that this book is situated outside of all Revelation, of all mystery, of all theology." [39]

In fact, the book develops casuistically, where all problems are envisaged as in a code from the point of view of the *permitted* and the *forbidden,* and where the search for possible cases is pushed to a ridiculous and odious extreme. Father Oraison cites some telling examples of the genre: "To kill oneself indirectly is *forbidden* in itself, but may be *permitted* for a proportionately serious motive. . . . This is why it is *permitted* to work in the blast furnaces, in the mines, in the glass works, in certain chemical plants, etc. . . . In the case of cancer, blood poisoning, etc., the amputation of a limb is *permitted.* . . . Conjugal relationships are *licit* when they are entered into with a view to the procreation of children or for another decent reason." But more to the point, there are indecent touches: "It is a grave sin to touch another person if such touches are made on indecent parts and without cause (even if it is only above the clothing) , whether it be made on a member of the same sex or not . . . touches on the less decent parts are ordinarily venial sins if done to a person of the same sex; on the other hand, if a member of the opposite sex is touched, it is ordinarily a mortal sin. The only exception is for touches that are completely superficial, done in frivolity or jest." [40]

It is evident that such a ridiculously serious teaching could in no way introduce an ethic of purity, but could quite well illustrate the Pauline affirmation: "Except through law I should never have become acquainted with sin. For example, I should never have known what it was to covet, if the law had not said, 'Thou shalt not covet'" (Rom. 7:7, NEB). These examples make us aware of how the necessities of the practice of confession and penance have determined this warping of ethics.

Father Oraison's book, which has the character both of a rough draft and a lampoon, shows to what extent such a moral teaching has raised lively reactions within Catholicism. Reactions were no less lively at the time of the Second Vatican Council, where the ethical teaching of the seminaries was harshly taken apart. But all these impassioned reactions have a theological background. During the past few decades, a whole series of works have appeared that have tried to reinsert ethics into a theology of grace. Such works have been based on Scripture as well as on a Thomistic base. We would mention in particular works such as Bernard Häring's *The Law of Christ*,[41] Schnackenburg's *Moral Teaching of the New Testament*,[42] Spicq's *Théologie morale du Nouveau Testament*,[43] and the work already mentioned by Pinckaers, *Le Renouveau de la morale*.

The increasing number of works of the same genre indicates that a profound change is taking place within Catholicism which concerns not only the appreciation of particular problems (social ethics, the problem of war, birth control), but which concerns the very foundation of ethics and the motivations of the ethical life. Rather than attempt to give an overall view of this renewal, and in order to keep our undertaking in the nature of an ecumenical confrontation, we shall now deal with the persistent divergences and the fortunate convergences between Catholic ethics and Protestant ethics.

II

THE PERSISTENT DIVERGENCES

Catholic ethics and Protestant ethics both are in flux and are undergoing a profound crisis. Both are in flux for the same reason: the fact that the structures of the world have changed, that man no longer conceives of his place in the world as he conceived of it for so long a time. In a relatively stable universe, man thought that it was possible and fairly easy to exercise his mastery, that is, of making prevail a certain number of values that seemed to him to express and assure his humanity, of exercising a certain number of virtues that were protected and encouraged by the social authorities. Now, today he perceives that social development is not governed by these values and these virtues, that it receives its dynamism and its finality from forces over which the personal subject has no hold.

These forces are primarily collective forces: nations, social classes, ideological blocs, and these realities evolve according to laws that are proper to them. It is not up to the subject to think of his place in the world independently of collective representations and the social mutations that operate outside of him. For example, how could one maintain an ideal of peace and concord if it is true, as Marxism teaches, that the primary force of progress is constituted by class warfare, by a permanent confrontation between reactionary groups and progressivist groups?

Besides these collective forces, even more anonymous

43

forces are at work: at least in one part of the world, technological developments have permitted the appearance of affluent societies, which also are societies of consumption, in which the primary imperative is to produce always more, to produce new objects, to create new needs, and to push forward a consumption always more varied and greater. In such a world, what becomes of the old Christian ideals of modesty, sobriety, and contentment with what one has?

On top of everything, in such a society the institution has become the dominant reality. Such a society can subsist and develop only by a certain planning in the economic, social, and cultural sectors. From this point, the individual initiatives which have been the great strength of Christendom seem to lose their value. The neighbor no longer is solely the one whom I encounter, with whom I form personal relationships, to whom I bear personal assistance. The neighbor can also be far away. The neighbor no longer can be solely a particular given individual, but such and such a social category (for example, laborers, migrants, the marginal professional categories, etc.) . For all these reasons, the problems of structure take a growing importance in ethical reflection. Moreover, social ethics takes a greater and greater place, whereas Christian tradition had centered ethics entirely on personal or interpersonal problems.

In these conditions, the churches meet with increasing difficulty in giving an ethical teaching which not only would be intelligible to modern man but would give him aid and light in the concrete problems that he lives. Such is the cause, or at least the occasion, of that profound alteration of ethics into which all the churches find themselves forced. And in this alteration is appears very clearly that the teaching so long perfected by ecclesiastical tradition, especially during the Scholastic period, has become outmoded. It was conditioned to a great extent by a social situation that no longer exists, by a state of out-of-date techniques. A return to the sources therefore has to go back

44

farther, toward the Bible and the patristic period. This is not because social conditioning did not operate at the level of the Biblical and patristic age, but because it is possible to disengage, especially from the Bible, certain requirements and inspirations tied to the apostolic kerygma, which can aid us in giving our present life an ethical significance. The return to the Bible is not done in a legalistic sense, as often is the case. It is not a question of transposing to our age certain prescriptions that had meaning only in relation to a definite historical situation. The Old Testament raises a warning against the concentration of the means of production, the creation of great capitalistic enterprises. It raises a warning against the proliferation of rules of law. Now, it is precisely the characteristic of our age that only the concentration of the means of production can assure the lowering of prices, the satisfaction of needs, and justice, and that the institutionalization of the forms of assistance, social prophylaxis, prevention, etc., require more and more numerous regulations, the extension of law to all forms of human activity. We will not find ready-made models of action in the Bible. But we may hope to find there a vision of man and of his destiny, a meaning and a finality to history which are precisely the elements that our present society is incapable of considering. This twofold search for an anthropology and for a vision of history (which naturally implies an eschatology) is no doubt the common objective of present-day Catholic and Protestant ethics. To be sure, they do not approach it in the same perspective and with the same presuppositions. Strong divergences continue to be evident.

1. *Nature and Supernature;*
   The Anthropological Problem

Catholic thought rightly subordinates ethics to anthropology. It justifiably affirms that only a vision of man can

45

clarify the ethical decision. This intention is affirmed in very clear fashion in the *Pastoral Constitution on the Church in the Modern World:* "In the light of Christ, the image of the unseen God, the firstborn of every creature, the Council wishes to speak to all men in order to illuminate the mystery of man and to cooperate in finding the solution to the outstanding problems of our time." [1]

But what image of man does Catholic teaching propose to us? It sees man under two aspects: man is a natural being and he also is a being with a supernatural vocation. Following the Thomist schema, man has in himself the superposition of a supernature over a nature. The role of a supernature is to fulfill the nature and lead it to perfection. Father Häring, in regard to love, illustrates this two-stage anthropology: *"Natural* love of self and of neighbor already has the foundation of the natural worth of the human person created in the image of God. This love attains its perfection only through grace in a supernatural surpassing. Supernatural love of self and of neighbor finds its foundation in a participation of grace in the nature of God (II Peter 1:4), in the call of divine love inviting us to this participation. Indeed, through charity, supernatural love, we do not love God solely as our Creator, we love him as our Father, with his own love, as he loves himself in the trinitarian intimacy. We know him in his Word of truth; we love him in his Spirit of love." [2] This text is quite significant: as creature of God, man, despite sin, does not cease to be the bearer of the image of God. Because he bears this image, because he is this image and is it by nature, he is capable of an ethical life. He can recognize the worth of the other. He can love the other, in the same way that he can love and know his Creator (since this is seen in non-Christian religions, especially in monotheistic religions, there is justification for the Catholic idea of an alliance and cooperation between the Catholic Church and these religions). But this natural man cannot go to the end of his own nature. In order to attain to the perfection of

46

this nature, it is necessary that a supernatural grace possess the natural man. Then love in itself is stripped of its limitations and its infirmities. Then love of God attains not only the Creator, but also the Father. Yet there is a continuity from the natural stage to the supernatural stage. There is not a true rupture between nature and supernature, but a surpassing. However, a certain doubt shows up at this point: the supernatural makes nature's desire a reality, but is nature conscious of this desire? Father Häring writes: "The natural love which refuses charity (or at least its implicit forms of absolute generosity) does not go to the end of the desire of nature. Only grace delivering us to the divine Persons fulfills this desire, at the very instant where it transcends it infinitely." [3] This last phrase seems to indicate an infinite qualitative difference between natural love and charity. But the beginning of the phrase seems to indicate that supernatural charity is implicitly contained in natural love. Yet charity, although it fulfills natural love, nevertheless has need of it: "Supernatural love of self and of neighbor, the love of charity, is situated by its value and its motives well above all natural love. And yet charity remains without great vigor if it cannot take up natural love. . . . It is charity itself which, from the pinnacle of the spirit (from the point of the soul), asks to descend into these sensible forces in order to capture the vigor of it." [4] Thus supernature, left to itself, would be without efficacy; it has need of finding the dynamism of the natural creature. Grace is capable of nothing without the nature that it fulfills. Redemption presupposes creation. It does not carry out a renewal of this creation, it does not substitute the new man for the old man: it carries the old creature to its perfection.

Moreover, it seems that supernature, despite its origin, is indeed an anthropological dimension. It inhabits the pinnacle of the spirit, the fine point of the soul, there at that point where nature has come to the peak of that which it can do by itself. It is infused in this soul: "True abnega-

47

tion of self is located in *the pinnacle of the spirit* and there is where takes place the most secret transformation of natural love into love informed by charity." [5]

This expression of pinnacle of the spirit or fine point of the soul (borrowed from mysticism, and very frequent in Meister Eckhardt) seems to indicate that natural man, who is himself conceived of as a hierarchized being (corporal life, sensible life, intellectual life, spiritual life), has a superior part that is predisposed to receive grace. In any case, it is there that supernature will insert itself into nature. All spirituality, in the human sense of this word, is in expectation of grace, which will come to complete it. Every soul is naturally Christian, perhaps not in fact, but by its confused expectation. It is the seat of the sighing of creation which awaits its redemption. This is undoubtedly the origin of the very intense interest, much more intense than in Protestantism, for all the forms of spirituality, for Hinduism, for the mystical currents of Islam.

A very important consequence for ethics results from this. Every ethic is specifically determined by its end, and this end, under whatever form it is presented, is always the full realization of the person, the completion of all his possibilities. "Now, in the name of the divine plan, human destiny, the end offered to man by God, is free and supernatural—participation in the divine life. And since it is the end which specifically determines ethics (for the latter is the conforming of acts to the end), man can have only one ethic, for he has only one end.

"Thus there is a possibility of two separate ethics for man: a purely human one and the other supernatural, and the first is assumed by the second. Naturally moral acts are put at the service of the supernatural life and given value by it. Although one speaks of natural morality, it will always be at the service of a destiny which surpasses it." [6]

The fact that the morality of the natural man is thus crowned and assumed while at the same time being integrated by supernatural morality justifies the claim of the

48

church to feel that it is the guardian of natural morality. Father Aubert states: "And from this fact, the church— founded by Christ and guardian of the supernatural order —is also guardian of the natural order; from the fact that man is a whole, ethically speaking as well as psychologically, the church, being charged with leading him to his true destiny, also has authority over natural morality." [7]

These considerations are not at all theoretical. They mean, for example, that at the level of social morality and of law, the church will take care always to maintain arrangements such that supernatural morality can come to extend and fulfill this natural morality. This may be illustrated by the Lateran Treaty which the Vatican signed with the fascist government of Mussolini. Despite the risks that it ran, and knew it ran, the Vatican did not hesitate to sign the Concordat, on condition that the indissolubility of marriage would be maintained in civil law, for this indissolubility seemed to the Vatican to be a guarantee of the possible insertion of the supernatural morality taught by the church.

Although Protestant rejection of natural morality is far from being unanimous, the rejection of the two-stage anthropology (with a communication by means of the fine point of the soul) is much more distinct. This is especially true currently, where substantialist language has largely been abandoned and where man is considered as an existence. Now, an existence does not divide. But since the Reformation, Protestant theology has tied the knowledge that man has of himself to his encounter with God. Man does not know himself in his authenticity except before God. And he then knows himself as *creature,* that is to say, as contingent reality called to existence by the free decision of the creator God. As Brunner points out: "To meet God the Lord means that we acknowledge that we are creatures. . . . The knowledge of God as Creator, and the knowledge of ourselves as creatures, are correlative truths." [8] Brunner adds that it is precisely in the degree that he does not encounter God, does not exist before God, that man is tempted, as the very work of his spiritual progress goes on, to distinguish within himself a nature and a supernature: the whole effort of ancient philosophical thought consisted precisely in rejecting the body to the realm of appearance, nothingness, inauthenticity. But not only the body—certain psychic functions were also rejected, for example, perception, imagination, sensibility. At the same time there was an effort to demonstrate the existence of an immortal, eternal, divine substance destined for participation in eternal realities. To say that man is a creature is to say that everything in him is creature: body, soul, and spirit. To be sure, man is not just any creature; he is distinguished from the other realities of creation. He, alone, of all living beings was created personally and not according to species; he, alone, of all the creatures was created in the image of God, but this image covers the totality of his being. It means that God has created man not as a thing which he can make use of, but as a being who can exist before him, who can be his partner, to whom he can address his word and who can respond to him. Creation itself is a covenant, and a covenant means that the partners undertake relationships. When one asserts, as the Reformers certainly tended to do, that this image of God has been totally destroyed by sin, and that it can only be restored, that is, created anew by faith in Christ, one forgets the fact that a negative response to God on the part of man is still formally a response: "Man will always respond to the call of the Creator." As Brunner writes: "Whatever kind of response man may make to the call of the Creator—in any case he does respond, even if his reply is: 'I do not know any Creator, and I will not obey any God.' Even this answer *is* an answer, and it comes under the inherent law of responsibility [i.e., the capacity to respond]. This formal essential structure cannot be lost." [9] And man responds with all his soul, with his body. The unity of the human being does not flag in any of his existential courses. Undoubtedly this unity is always a fragile unity, due to sin. But man knows that he exists only at this price and this is why the desire for unity characterizes all his steps. Engagement, which characterizes the moral life, is nothing other than the recuperation, at least in the attempt, of this unity, in order that action express the being in his unity. This unity appears in eminent fashion in the man justified by grace. The fruit of this grace is that he becomes capable of offering his body, that is to say, the totality of his person in living sacrifice, holy and agreeable to God (Rom. 12:1). No distinction between nature and supernature appears in all of this. To be sure, it is by grace that man becomes thus capable of a total engagement, of the manifestation of an existential unity. But, precisely, grace does not constitute a supernature. It does not become an anthropological element. It remains a gift which is never separated from the giver, which exists only in the act of the giver.

Furthermore, the justified man, the reconciled man, the man beyond judgment remains a creature who participates certainly in the Trinitarian life in the person of Christ, the firstborn of all creation. But man is by no means divinized. It is by Christ made man, clothed forever in his humanity, that man is rendered a participant in the mysterious life of the persons of the Trinity. Such is the theological significance of the ascension. Now, Catholic theology, following the Greek fathers and Saint Augustine, teaches the doctrine of *theiosis* or of *theiopoesis* which it considers to be the translation of the Pauline doctrine of filial adoption and of II Peter 1:4 ("to share in the very being of God," NEB). The completion of nature by a supernature ends thus in the divinization of man, as if redemption could call into question the very meaning of creation: in the act of creation, God has not engendered a replica of himself. He called into being a being different from himself, a being called to enter into communion with him, but not to become identified with him.

51

This profound difference in the anthropology which reflects on the doctrine of man's destination has certain consequences from an ethical point of view. To elucidate these consequences, we need only to refer to the doctrine of love. We have seen that Catholic theologians make a distinction, both qualitative and intensive, between natural love—sympathetic or friendly—and charitable love, but at the same time, they represent the former as a sort of receptacle awaiting perfectioning by the latter. They make a distinction, but only in order to unite, and the distinction does not hinder a continuity being established by the intervention of grace. Protestant theologians see a distinction of quite a different type between Eros and Agape. This distinction is also much more radical. For it is a difference of essence, and Eros cannot be fulfilled in Agape. It can only surrender its claims to Agape. According to Anders Nygren,[10] Eros is the desire for the best. This best can be God himself and through Eros, man attempts to divinize himself, which is sin itself. Eros is motivated by the quality of the object that it seeks to possess. It turns aside from what appears valueless to it. Such is what its possessive character exacts. It is always centripetal.

Agape, on the contrary, is the gift of the self, which is not determined by the worth of the object, and that is where it is freedom and grace. It creates the value of the loved being, far rather than being determined by a pre-existent value. It is manifested in divine election. The historical inquiry of Nygren tends to show that pagan philosophy in its highest expressions (for example, in Platonism) knew only Eros and was ignorant of Agape. Love as Plato describes it in *The Banquet* consists in an ascending dialectic by which we lift ourselves up from the love of beautiful bodies to the love of beautiful forms, to the love of mathematical harmony, and finally, to the love of ideas. And in the course of this ascension, we divinize ourselves. Through love, the soul is awakened to the desire for absolute perfection in order to possess it. The soul thus witnesses that it is in love with itself. Agape, on the contrary, is specifically and exclusively a Christian idea. Here love is a descending movement. It starts from God and goes toward man. It is not motivated by the worth of man, for man is a miserable thing and a sinner. He is not lovable in himself. Coming from a God who has no need of men (Plato explained Eros by a want, a poverty), it is entirely gratuitous and disinterested. When man knows himself loved with this love, then he is impelled in turn to love his neighbor in himself in disinterested fashion, even if this neighbor is hostile ("Love your enemies"). No compromise is possible between these two types of love. They are two different essences. Saint Augustine was wrong in wanting to seek an impossible synthesis, which he termed *caritas* and which, in reality, is only a hybrid reality mixing New Testament Agape with Greek Eros. This example is prolonged in all the medieval theologies.

In order to give Nygren's analyses their true import, it is necessary to see that he attempted to distinguish essences and that he did not undertake a psychological investigation. By that is meant that in the concrete love of a Christian, we are not going to find Agape in its pure state. We will always find it cropping out, for better or for worse, right smack in the middle of Eros. What is incompatible on the level of essence coexists on the level of lived experience, without its being possible to make a clear distinction, to separate the good grain from the chaff before harvest time. So the new man destined for eternal life and the old man destined for death coexist in the person without its ever being possible to disassociate them. Yet what is certain is that Agape must fight in order to triumph over Eros and that it does not fulfill Eros. It is the very principle of Eros as captor and possessor, and ultimately, as love of self that must be extirpated. Or if one wishes, Eros, just like the old man, must pass through a death and a resurrection. Without this death, there will be no spontaneous transfiguration of Eros, no development of Eros in an Agape

53

which repudiates it.[11]

Thus, on one hand, the supernatural is not an anthropological dimension for Protestant ethics; the human being in his wholeness and in his unity is a natural being, a creature. Grace must seize hold of this being in its entirety. But, on the other hand, it never seizes hold of this being without leading him through a dying to himself, without burying him by baptism in the death of Christ. Supernature does not come to complete and perfect a nature which would have need only of a complement, of an increase of soul as Bergson said. On the contrary, it comes to transform it, in the strict sense of the word, to reorient it toward a completely different finality. But this reorientation is possible only through the death of the sinner-being.

2. *The Problem of Natural Law and of Natural Morality*

This problem obviously is tied to the preceding problem: the duality of nature and of supernature corresponds to the two primary sources of ethics, natural divine law and supernatural divine law (or positive law, or revealed law). Whatever be the growing part given to revealed law by contemporary Catholic moral theology, it has always affirmed that revealed morality presupposes natural morality while at the same time surpassing it and fulfilling it. Do these two aspects of morality correspond to the two aspects of the work of God: creation and redemption? Not completely. "For, in fact, man has never existed with his nature alone," writes Aubert. "From the time of his creation, in an act of gracious benevolence, God called him to a destiny surpassing the Creator-creature relationship, in order to introduce him into the intimacy of the divine life, inviting him to participate in this divine life with all that means of knowledge and happiness. The theologians express that truth in saying that man has been created by God

54

in a supernatural state, that is to say, absolutely surpassing the tendencies and requirements of simple human nature. . . . Man's original state was not nature in its totality; participation in the divine nature does not belong to that properly natural state without which man is not man." [12] Sin has struck primarily at supernature, depriving man of his intimate state with God. It has not corrupted nature in its foundation, but "it has not left human nature in the state of simplicity and integrity that it bears in and of itself." [13] Thus when we speak of a natural morality, it is not a question of a moral system valid for man in his *status integritatis;* it involves a morality for a man whose nature undoubtedly has been wounded by the Fall, but whose essential nature has remained what it was, although without its normal extension in a supernature.

When pontifical texts evoke this natural morality and the natural law which arises from it, they are referring to a morality and a law which flow from the nature of things and primarily from human nature, as we have just characterized it: an integrity, to be sure, but only if one abstracts from the fact that it is no longer completed in its supernatural extension. The content of this morality and this law concern primarily the family, property, work, society, the state, that is to say, precisely those realities that have an existence independent of redemption, that have an existence in non-Christian societies as well as in Christian societies. Although this morality and this law have their definitive origin in God, reason with its natural lights can discover the principal aspects of human nature and consequently formulate the primary requirements of natural law. Thus the latter constitutes a common language for all reasonable beings, the indispensable base for the constitution of a human community in which Christians and non-Christians may live together. Natural law in its objective requirements, though of course not in all the local and historical particularities of positive law, remains valid for all men in all ages. It constitutes the infrastructure of all social life and provides a common denominator for dialogue between Christians and non-Christians. But natural morality is not, for all that, without relation to revealed morality. This is true not only because revealed morality always presupposes natural morality (Jesus in his teaching refers to the Second Tablet of the Decalogue, which by its content is of natural law), but also because, as nature is completed by and extends into supernature, so natural morality summons revealed morality for which it prepares the way.

It is not by chance that marriage, the basic institution of natural law, can become in Scripture the symbol of the supernatural union of Christ with his church. The indissolubility of marriage, which, we are told, would be an exigence of nature, considering the necessities of procreation, of the education of children, and of natural assistance that the parents owe, receives a new illumination when, through revelation, marriage becomes an analogy of the tie uniting Christ to his church. Then the indissolubility ceases to be a reasonable and useful juridical principle, and becomes the expression of the faithfulness of love: "The simple source of human flowering, it [marriage] becomes the source of grace by its elevation to the rank of sacrament." [14]

While asserting that natural law constitutes the means of communication between men and the means for the establishment of a human nonconfessional society, the Catholic Church is thus led to think that because it holds in reserve a supernatural revelation, it is much better able than unbelievers to read and interpret correctly the natural law.

"The knowledge of the natural law is possible by the forces of reason alone, but often with how many difficulties and imperfections. On the contrary, thanks to the light of Revelation, the prescriptions of this law receive a new illumination which thereby manifests the narrow and vital relationship that reigns between the natural order and that issuing from the gospel." [15]

This position of strength which the Catholic Church

feels it holds (it knows better than unbelievers that which they should know themselves had they not repudiated the use of reason) has, in reality, become extremely tenuous for two reasons. On the one hand, humane sciences such as sociology and ethnology have disclosed to us such a great variety of perfectly contradictory moral practices and conceptions that it becomes difficult to perceive the expression of this universal (and undoubtedly already Christianized) natural morality which Christianity teaches. How do we decide that polygamy is less natural than monogamy; that the right of personal property is natural law, whereas in the past history of mankind we find the right of property essentially under a collective form; that a great part of humanity is heading toward the socialization of the means of production and exchange?

On the other hand, certain doctrines, notably Marxism, whose rational structures are undeniable, systematically call into question the principles of natural morality and law concerning work, the family, property, and the state. One can understand the disarray Marxism has thrown Catholic thought into. Far from constituting only a danger for the traditional social order, Marxism represents a form of Western-born rational thought, rooted in a classical tradition, and which relativizes the norms of natural law by showing that they are nothing other than the products of social conditions, which themselves are a reflection of the relations of production. One can see why it has taken nearly a century for the Catholic Church to accept the need to give positive attention to a doctrine that is primarily a sort of intellectual and moral scandal to Catholicism.[16]

The Catholic Church, although its theology tries to take account of the attainments of science as well as of the Marxist critique, continues to utilize the idea of natural law. The great social encyclicals of John XXIII, *Mater et Magistra* (1961) and *Pacem in Terris* (1963), are constructed on a significant schema; all the theses upheld,

57

which often are quite bold, are based primarily on the arguments of natural law and of reason, and are then supported by Scriptural arguments which thus come to clarify and consolidate the base of natural law. (This structure, moreover, is more manifest in the second encyclical than in the first.) *Pacem in Terris,* from the beginning, recalls the norms of conduct inscribed in human nature. The respect due to the human person, the right of benefiting from the goods of culture, like the right of honoring God according to the just requirement of the correct conscience, the right of property, the ontological and teleological priority of the individual over society—all belong to natural law. Even the right of collective bargaining comes from natural law (*Mater et Magistra*) .

It is true that the concept of natural law loses some of its precision when it is given such amplitude. Indeed, all the laws that mankind has uncovered in the course of its development, all the values that society, in a particular historical situation, has been led to unveil and give preference to are attached in more or less arbitrary fashion to the natural law. The content of this law seems essentially to be variable. Although John XXIII maintained, with *Rerum Novarum,* that the right of private ownership of the goods of production is an inalienable right, depending on human nature, he tends nevertheless to limit and counterbalance this right by a socialization that effectively appears as a necessity in the industrial societies. And it is not very clear how this socialization accords with the ontological and teleological priority of the individual over society. Throughout *Mater et Magistra* one perceives a kind of nostalgia for familial work, which John XXIII always considered to be the most reasonable and most beneficent form in the agricultural domain.

A development seems to be taking place, however, which was indicated when it was revealed that the conciliar constitution *Gaudium et Spes* had readily rejected the use of arguments of natural law. The entire anthropology pre-

58

sented there intends to be strictly Scriptural. Moreover, it was stated that this new method was meant to facilitate the development of the ecumenical dialogue with the churches of the Reformation. The new method chosen would thus be connected with a tactic, in the best sense of the word, or with a pedagogy. But even though it was a matter of ecumenical pedagogy, does not the fact that it is possible to present the social ethic of the church for the contemporary world without basing it on natural law tend to prove that natural law does not constitute an indispensable structure for Catholic ethics?

As Protestants are clearly hostile regarding a Thomist type of anthropology which introduces into man a nature completed by and fulfilled in a supernature, and as they are hesitant and divided over the problem of natural law and natural morality, so are they in regard to natural theology. Although in our day the thought of Karl Barth is characterized by categorical rejection of all natural theology and of all natural morality, although Barth himself has attempted to construct an ethics based solely on the freedom which is given to us in Christ, this orientation is far from being accepted by all the theologians. The resistance is particularly strong among Lutherans and among strict Calvinists. Moreover, an exegete as informed about Barth as Father Bouillard has shown that in Barth's anthropology as well as in his ethics, there is a more or less clandestine use of ideas that arise, not from the Word of God, but from the analysis of the permanent structures of man. Father Bouillard shows in a certain number of precise examples (marriage, respect for life, work) that Barth proceeds to a direct deciphering of the meaning of human situations, that he makes an appeal in his analysis to reason more than to revelation. When Barth teaches us that man must respect his own life, including the instinctive life, and then adds that one must not abandon himself to his instincts but rather must dominate and control them by free and reasonable decisions, he is saying something that is quite cor-

59

rect. However, he induces them. For example, he claims that the fact of the birth of Christ, "which unveils the eternal love of God for man, makes manifest that human life has a sacred character." [17]

Revelation, Father Bouillard tells us, concerns the knowledge of justified man. Certainly it clarifies the knowledge that we have of man before his justification. It does not constitute it entirely. For, as the existence of the humane sciences proves, we are capable, outside of all reference to revelation, of disengaging the structures of human existence. And quite often the knowledge of these structures aids us in deciphering revelation itself. Do we not better understand the account of the creation of man and woman in Genesis, now that we have better unveiled the psychological structures of the man-woman relationship and have given increased value to the sexual relationship itself?

On the other hand, André Dumas, in a study entitled "La Théologie de Karl Barth et le droit naturel," [18] shows that in Barth's thought itself there is a sort of equivalence of natural law, namely, the Christological analogies.

Certainly, Barth rejects quite strenuously the Catholic idea of natural law, which, it seems to him, quite correctly, is rooted in the idea of natural revelation. Civil society and the state are, in his eyes, spiritually blind, since all knowledge of God comes from the Word of God. When the church wants to intervene in the social and political life, it cannot have recourse to this natural law. "If it does," Barth writes, "the Christian community would show that it does not fear appropriating the methods proper to the civil community . . . without taking account of the center of gravity upon which they both depend." (Barth feels that the church and the civil society are not two great giants side by side, but two concentric realities, equally subject to Christ, which the church knows but which the civil society is ignorant of.) Barth claims that if the church were to do this, "it would put itself in tow of the pagan state. In that

60

case, the Christian community no longer would be capable
of fulfilling its specific function in the midst of the civil
society; it no longer would be the salt and the light that it
is called to be within this larger circle. Instead of simply
declaring itself interdependent with the civil community,
it would in fact identify itself with it, and precisely in that
which it lacks. Thus the Christian community could no
longer render it the least service." [19]

Certainly, Barth recognizes clearly that the civil society
can only refer itself to a so-called natural law, although it
appears to him to be like a historical reality, relative and
variable, like an effort of reason to determine the just and
the unjust: "And the civil community as such—that which
has not yet been or no longer is enlightened by He who
occupies its center—undoubtedly has no other choice but
to learn, somehow or other, to think, to speak, and to act,
on the basis of the givens of this law, that is to say, on the
basis of the conception which one has of it following the
period of history." [20] Barth certainly is correct in thinking
that natural law is confused quite often with a sort of juridical positivism that is content to ratify *de facto* sociological developments.

But, given the fact that the church which wants to address itself to the world must deal with natural, profane
problems, and can do it only in a language that is not Biblical or ecclesiastical, that is, if it does not wish to remain
totally misunderstood by non-Christians, given this, what
does Barth propose to us as a counterresponse? "The orientation of Christian political action, an action that consists in a discernment, a judgment, a law, a will, and a com-
mitment, is in relationship with the twofold nature of the
state, which possesses both the faculty of furnishing and
the need of receiving an analogous image of the Kingdom
of God which the church proclaims." [21] Although the state
can be confused neither with the church nor with the Kingdom, it cannot be considered theologically in a fashion independent of them. In an eschatological perspective, the

61

state is a sort of image of the Kingdom. This is why it must or should furnish an analogy of it. It is capable, given its destiny, of being an analogy or a parable of the Kingdom. However, because of its spiritual blindness, it does not succeed in being such a parable. This is why all politics becomes debased. "In order to preserve the civil community from decadence and ruin," Barth maintains, "it is necessary for it to be reminded again and again of the demands of that justice which it is held to represent. The civil community thus has *need of analogy* as much as it is capable of forming an analogy.[22] . . .

"The Christian community thus calls the civil community to forsake its attitude of neutrality, of spiritual indifference, of its natural paganism, in order to engage with the Christian community, before God, in a policy of shared coresponsibility. In becoming political, the Christian community thus manifests its faithfulness to its mission in that which is most authentic to it. The community starts in motion the movement of history whose end and content must be to make the earthly city a parable, an analogical sign of the Kingdom of God, by enabling it to fulfill the tasks of civil justice." [23]

Thus analogy takes the place of natural law as the basis of the church's intervention in political and profane life. Starting with the gospel, the church must discover and invent parables which express the demands of the gospel in the civil society. Thus the church, knowing the mercy of God, who in Jesus Christ became man, will ask that the civil community devote its attention to man rather than to things. Thus the church, knowing that the Son of Man came to seek and save those who are lost, will be insistent that politics give priority attention to those economically weak, or that legislation make compensation for the social inequalities. Thus the church, knowing that men are called to freedom, will give its preference to a regime of freedom and not to a tyranny, etc., etc.

These wise directives result thus in the giving of privi-

62

leged status to a certain number of secular social and political values which Catholic theology would say are of
natural law. But the difference does not bear on the content of these values. For Barth, they are parables of the
coming Kingdom. It is *eschatological* illumination which
gives them their value, while at the same time forbidding
their absolutizing, making idols of them (which is the ordinary temptation of politics). For Catholic natural-law
theologians, these values have an *ontological* foundation,
in the sense that they belong to an order of creation and
remain unblemished in spite of the sinful history in which
they are engaged.

As A. Dumas has correctly observed: "In the first case
(i.e., that of the theology of natural law), nature is in substantial convergence with revelation. In spite of sin, in
spite of the passions, in spite of the distance between the
original order and the reality of the present, nature bears
in itself a rational and vital substratum that founds natural
law, as the church helps it to be clarified. . . . In the second case, nature converges eschatologically with revelation.
Nature moves toward the time in which the particularity
of the church will disappear in favor of the universality
of the city of God." [24]

Catholic moral theology seeks a foundation in an original and ontological given, which seems difficult to grasp.
It is also led to call certain exigences eternal which in fact
are relative and sociologically conditioned (for example,
the right of ownership and, a few centuries ago, the divine
right of kings). Protestant moral thought, on the other
hand, seeks its foundation in an eschatological hope, which,
by the weight that it exercises over the present, calls for
an incessant renewal of social structures and legislations.
This profound difference could explain why Catholic
moral theology tends to be rather more conservative,
whereas Protestant moral thought would rather insist more
on the criticism of the established order, on the hopes for
justice on the part of the dissatisfied. For the one thinks

that the starting point is an original past, which it believes is substantially one with revelation, whereas the other thinks that the starting point is a future that approaches and that we now prepare signs or parables of that which is promised us.

Thus Catholic ethics for centuries has condemned interest-bearing loans, claiming that money—the artificial creation of man—is void of any power of production, whereas land, a natural reality, is naturally productive and should give a yield. Protestant ethics has authorized interest-bearing loans, to the degree that the production of new wealth by this means permits the expansion of man's reign. Such expansion also is a parable (however ambiguous) of the plenitude of the Kingdom.

However, and despite these divergences, we should also point out a *rapprochement:* whether we speak of natural law, ontologically grounded, or of Christological analogies which take their significance from the eschatological Kingdom, in both cases it is evident that moral theory, in order to express itself and to become reality, will have need of values that are not necessarily contained as such in the Biblical revelation. The idea of the responsible society which the World Council of Churches puts forward to clarify our social and political problems is not a Biblical idea. It is the equivalent neither of the ecclesial community nor of the community of the Kingdom. It is an analogy valid for secular times, for a secularized society. These values that ethics is led to discover can have a meaning independent of their Christological links. They can be understood and accepted by the non-Christian to the degree that he perceives that they can contribute to the creation of a more just secular order. It is possible and desirable for Christians and non-Christians to understand each other on the requirements of a just peace at a given moment in history, although for Christians this social peace is the reflection and the proclamation of things to come and although for non-Christians this same peace exhausts itself in the temporal happiness that it permits.

While recognizing that ethics has need of making reference to common values, although seen in the perspective of the faith in an intentionality of which reason is ignorant, Protestant ethics will maintain against Catholic ethics that there is no need of having recourse to a natural law, under the pretext that natural law would be more universal and thus of a human import far vaster than the evangelical requirements, as if the gospel represented a sort of particular reality in the midst of natural law. It is necessary to maintain that Biblical revelation is the disclosure of universality, that it makes known universal man, that is to say, the human condition, better than a natural law which refers to a nontemporal and imperceptible nature and to a reason that is incorrectly postulated not to have a history. Although the values which serve to mediate Christian ethics and which can indeed be understood by every thinking man are an indispensable instrument of every ethic, they do not satisfactorily disclose the condition of man *semper peccator et semper justus.*

3. *The Meaning of Secularization*

Catholic ethics and Protestant ethics remain divergent in their appreciation of the civil society and its function as well as in the appreciation of the relationships that should be established between church and civil society, church and state. These divergences appear in clearest fashion in the attitude taken toward a sociological development which has been determinative, especially in the West, for the form and structure of civil society and the awareness that the civil society has of itself. This development is called secularization. By that is meant the process which eventuated in the liquidation of medieval Christendom, of the intimate union between the civil society and the religious society, and of the control that the church exercised over the primary forms of human activity, cultural, artistic, political, juridical, and even economic. This Christendom has come undone, the two societies have ceased to coincide and to interpenetrate. This began when it became possible, with the unity of faith no longer existing, to belong to the civil society without belonging to the church. From that moment, the various spheres of human activity were able to become increasingly secularized, that is to say, they could affirm their autonomy in relation to ecclesiastical control. Science was the first to manifest its independence from theology, art ceased to be exclusively a sacred art, the center of authority in politics no longer originated and functioned in the control of the church, and economy began to follow its own laws, and was increasingly in close conjunction with technological development and increasingly less concerned with the ineffective regulations of the church. The law is a good representative of this development. The law, which in the Middle Ages was the law established and universalized by the church, had largely separated from canonical prescriptions to the point of contradicting them (freedom of thought, divorce, etc.). Thus secularization appeared as a process of dissociation between the two societies, civil and religious. But this dissociation was also accompanied by a continuous growth of the powers of the civil society and the state, and of their social functions. The church and the churches, either *de facto* or by virtue of juridical provisions, found themselves circumscribed within the realm of the spiritual, of the care of souls, of the organization of worship. Secularization, then, is a phenomenon of the reflux of religion from the public domain to the private domain. It is characterized by the tendency of the churches to become marginal societies after long having controlled, inspired, and crowned the totality of social life. This private sector, in which the churches would be privileged to carry on their activities, would at the same time grow smaller due to the fact that many functions traditionally performed by the individual or the family passed

66

into the hands of society and that a great part of individual existence (work and leisure time) became socialized. Bonhoeffer correctly describes the secularization process when he summarizes it as follows: "The displacement of God from the world, and from the public part of human life, led to the attempt to keep his place secure at least in the sphere of the 'personal,' the 'inner,' and the 'private.' And as every man still has a private sphere somewhere, that is where he was thought to be the most vulnerable." [25]

To be sure, this phenomenon of secularization is not entirely identical with that of dechristianization. The churches can very well not accept this marginal place that is prepared for them. They can seek new means of action in the global society; they can inform public opinion. But they have recourse to procedures that are far different from those available to them when they occupied an official and dominant place in state and society.

The Catholic Church, which is strongly impregnated with the archetype of Christendom, has never completely accepted the idea of secularization. It would be inexact to say that it has not accepted the idea at all. For a long time it has practiced and still practices the policy of concordats. Now, in the modern era, to the degree that concordats no longer postulate that the state is Christian and that the state should not work, at least directly, in the salvation of souls, that church and state cooperate—toward an end, of course, but an end that is far off and that in the immediate there is a very clear differentiation of functions between church and state—to this degree, concordats indeed signify a recognition of secularization. They seek simply to ward off certain troublesome effects of this situation. The church asks the state to guarantee it certain public liberties, certain immunities, and certain services necessary to the accomplishment of its own mission, and, on the other hand, the church agrees that it will undertake no action that could hinder the state in the fulfillment of its own mission. The Catholic Church has not been content to sign concordats with so-called Christian states; it has signed them, and is always disposed to do so, with states that are confessionally neutral. According to Desqueyrat and Halbecq, "For a state to sign a concordat, it is not necessary that it subscribe to the canons of the Council of Trent, nor even to the Decalogue; it is sufficient for it to recognize the church as a society of public international law." [26] To conclude a concordat with a state that has ceased to be Christian, or even, as has also happened, with an anti-Christian totalitarian state, is to take note of secularization, to draw out its consequences, and to find a *modus vivendi* with a secularized society.

But, for all that, the Catholic Church itself has not accepted the principles of secularization. It continues to see it as a sort of misfortune for humanity. And although the church has ceased to prescribe for science the limits in which it should operate, it nonetheless seeks a sometimes facile concordism between the teaching that it gives and science, if science manifests something of interest for spiritual problems. In this regard, one could say that the thought of Teilhard de Chardin, although it surely presents nonnegligible dangers for Catholic orthodoxy, has a good chance of being widely accepted by the church. For it permits a demonstration that theology is still capable of assuming and inspiring modern science. Although the church has given up seeing its canonical principles applied by the states, it nevertheless attempts to preserve some bridgeheads of canon law in secular legislation (for example, legislation on divorce). Although the church has given up contesting the autonomy of culture, at least it tries either to operate private education concurrently with that of a non-Christian state or to maintain the confessionalism of education everywhere that it is possible.

The clearest condemnation of secularization (although the word was not then used in the same sense) is obviously contained in Pius IX's encyclical *Quanta Cura* and in the *Syllabus* which is annexed to it (1864). One reads in this

68

encyclical: "Men are not lacking today who apply to the civil society the impious and absurd principle of *Naturalism,* as they call it. They dare to teach that the perfection of governments and civil progress absolutely require that the human society be constituted and be governed without any longer taking account of religion, as if it no longer existed, or at least without making any difference between the true religion and the false. Moreover, contrary to the doctrine of Scripture, of the Church, and of the Holy Fathers, they are not afraid of asserting that the best government is that in which one no longer recognizes that the authority has the obligation of repressing, under pain of punishment, those who attack the Catholic religion, if it is not when public peace demands it . . .

"When religion is separated from the civil society, the doctrine and the authority of divine revelation are rejected, the true idea of justice and of human law are obscured and lost . . . and physical force takes the place of justice and true law. . . . Do not neglect either to teach that kingly power is not conferred solely for the governing of this world, but above all for the protection of the Church."

Of course, from Pius IX to Paul VI, the Catholic Church has come a long way. One will notice that the encyclicals of John XXIII and the pastoral constitution *Gaudium et Spes* make no allusion to the problem of secularization, and do not call for a Christian society in which religion would occupy a predominant place. Quite the contrary, *Gaudium et Spes* seems indeed to admit that a certain social pluralism is desirable: "Many different people go to make up the political community, and these can lawfully incline toward diverse ways of doing things. Now, if the political community is not to be torn to pieces as each man follows his own viewpoint, authority is needed. This authority must dispose the energies of the whole citizenry toward the common good, not mechanically or despotically, but primarily as a moral force which depends on freedom and the conscientious discharge of the burdens of any office. . . . It is therefore obvious that the political community and public authority are based on human nature and hence belong to an order of things divinely foreordained. At the same time, the choice of government and the method of selecting leaders is left to the free will of citizens." [27] We see that the church recognizes the political community's autonomy in regard to it. It claims no other right than that of teaching freely, of spreading its ethical doctrine in regard to man and the social life.

Has the Catholic Church, then, lost all nostalgia for Christendom, or does it rather consider secularization as a makeshift thing to which it must accommodate itself? In a dialogue between Father Daniélou and Jean Bosc in regard precisely to the Constitution *Gaudium et Spes,* the Protestant speaker asked Father Daniélou on several occasions what amounted to the question whether the Catholic Church still does not persist in the idea of Christianizing the social structures (which is the main aspect of the regime of Christendom) and whether it still does not confuse the cause of the gospel with the interests of a Christian civilization. Several of Father Daniélou's answers are significant: "There is something that strikes me in what you've said. It undoubtedly is related to a difference in the structures of our theologies. Basically, you pose the question in two terms: on the one hand, the gospel, and on the other, temporal civilization. Certainly, I interject an intermediary element, which is that of the religious dimension of man as such." [28] This means that for the Catholic theologian, although there is indeed a necessary distinction between the world and the church, he does not agree that this world which is distinct from the church is entirely secularized. He discovers in the world a sort of mediation between the secular and Christian faith, this mediation being the religious dimensions. Whereas the Protestant theologian has the tendency, especially in modern times, to see a form of idolatry in religion, a system which tends to dispose relationships between sacred and profane in such a

70

way that man can enter into contact with the sacred with the least possible risk (and sometimes, as with Karl Barth, we find pure and simple incredulity), Catholic thought continues to consider that religion, the expression of the original nature of man, constitutes an indispensable foundation for the insertion of Christianity: "For my part," Father Daniélou writes, "it seems impossible to me to think that a civilization is truly human to the degree that religious values are not represented in it. These religious values appear to me as constituents of the very civilization, that is to say, that a civilization in which religious values are not represented is an inhuman civilization, where man is not represented in his totality. I understand religion in a very general sense . . . not so much as existing religions as of a certain dimension of every man, of which, moreover, the only fully valid interpretation is found in Jesus Christ." [29] In other words, Father Daniélou does not accept the idea of a purely secularized civilization. He does not agree that outside of faith in the living God, there is only profane reality. Compare these affirmations with those of a Bonhoeffer, for example, who thinks, on the contrary, that the great opportunity of Christianity, thanks to secularization, is to be a nonreligious Christianity, that is to say, which no longer supports itself on a previous religion and where faith can be only the decisive leap that brings one from incredulity to the confession of the crucified Lord. Bonhoeffer describes in these terms the secularization which goes back properly speaking to the thirteenth century and shows at the same time that it is of no value for the Christian faith to try to save any vestiges from the age anterior to secularization: "Man has learnt to deal with himself in all questions of importance without recourse to the 'working hypothesis' called 'God.' In questions of science, art, and ethics this has become an understood thing at which one now hardly dares to tilt. . . . It is becoming evident that everything gets along without 'God'—and, in fact, just as well as before. As in the scientific field, so in

71

human affairs generally, 'God' is being pushed more and more out of life, losing more and more ground.

"The attack by Christian apologetic on the adulthood of the world I consider to be in the first place pointless, in the second place ignoble, and in the third place unchristian. Pointless, because it seems to me like an attempt to put a grown-up man back into adolescence, i.e., to make him dependent on things on which he is, in fact, no longer dependent, and thrusting him into problems that are, in fact, no longer problems to him. Ignoble, because it amounts to an attempt to exploit man's weakness for purposes that are alien to him and to which he has not freely assented. Unchristian, because it confuses Christ with one particular stage in man's righteousness, i.e., with a human law." [30]

This religious civilization of which Father Daniélou speaks would be a civilization in which the idea would be maintained that somewhere there is a Supreme Power, a transcendence that should inspire fear in man, and that would thus limit man's freedom and majority. But what relationship would there be between this Supreme Power, this First Cause which would limit man, and the God hidden in Jesus Christ, the only true God who affirms his presence in that which is quite the opposite of a power, in the Suffering Servant, the crucified One? Can one really pass from one to the other without the leap of faith? If we maintain a place for God in the universe of physics, as Descartes did, by asserting that only the immutability of God guarantees the constancy in the universe of the quantity of movement (which, moreover, was a scientifically false proposition), does one really believe that this will render faith easier for the scientists? The appeal of the gospel, if it is to be heard, must be addressed to an alienated man, maintained in a state of puerility by a more or less superstitious fear of an obscure power—or has it no more chance of being heard in its authenticity by an adult man, master and possessor of nature and to the degree possible

72

for him, who would then freely sacrifice his majority and power before the crucified Christ? This dependence maintained in a poorly secularized world in regard to obscure religious powers, which in reality are false gods, is undoubtedly a state of infancy—and in order to give this state value and priority, some would quote Christ's word: "Whoever does not accept the kingdom of God like a child will never enter it" (Mark 10:15). But they forget that this word is addressed to adults, that it does not mean: Guard against growing up, remain in your puerility. On the contrary, it means: You who are adults, become again like little children. The secularized world is the world of adults, of those who have rejected religious terrors, the feeling of absolute dependence of their childhood. It is for these men that the gospel has a meaning. If, because of a poorly secularized world, one maintained even slightly a confusion between the God formed in our image, the God of the religious dimension of man, and the God of the gospel, one certainly will become involved in ambiguities: one will make Christianity one religion among others and especially will one make Christianity an indispensable function of society, but due to these equivocations, the specific nature of the gospel will be in danger of being obscured and the misunderstanding will continue concerning the difference between gospel and religion.

This is one of the major sources of divergence between Catholic ethics and Protestant ethics. Let us recognize, however, that Protestant theology is far from being unanimous on this point. The current represented by Barth and Bonhoeffer is not the only current. One will find many positions in Protestantism that, on this point, are similar to the Catholic position. We are thinking in particular here of the thought of Tillich. Tillich, no matter how far he may be from Catholicism on other points, nevertheless comes close to Catholicism in his concern to discover a religious dimension in all the forms of civilization and culture, a search for what he calls "ultimate reality." Where-ever this concern for ultimate reality exists, Tillich feels that an ontological question is being posed, to which only the Christian revelation brings an adequate response. In all his studies of science, art, and culture, Tillich attempted to show that all these disciplines pose the question of God. Thus he shows a great apologetical interest in all forms of civilization which maintain the search for ultimate reality, which therefore are not entirely secularized, even when they believe themselves to be.[31] Unfortunately, only Christianity can make such a reading of civilization and culture that the search for ultimate reality, from the depths of being, in no way predisposes to the reception of the Christian response. This is seen in the most lucid thinkers who are consciously anti-Christian, such as Heidegger.

The Catholic attachment to an incompletely secularized society is expressed on the social and political level by attitudes which are clearly different from those common to Protestantism, in particular, by the rejection of political and educational nonconfessionalism. The Catholic Church certainly does not ask the state to be Christian. It knows that that is impossible, and is appreciative in proper measure of the Catholicism of a Franco or a Salazar. But it does ask the state to be religious. It means for the state to respect the God of natural revelation, and attempts an impossible dissociation between the first and the second article of the Creed. It does not ask that the school be a substitute for the church, that the school teach the Catechism; it would be sufficient for the school to teach the duties toward the Creator.

Another thing that one sees, and this was very evident at the time of the Council's discussion on non-Christian religions, is an attempt to find a contact, perhaps an alliance, with the great monotheistic religions, those which in its eyes have received the benefit of natural theology. This contact is sought with a view to preserving civilization from any infiltration of atheism. The idea of a league against

74

atheism is never entirely absent from Roman policy. Indeed, it is this idea that undoubtedly constitutes one of the major points on which the Catholic Church and the World Council of Churches disagree. This was the feeling behind Visser 't Hooft's statement that "Christians or Christian churches could not agree without qualification to collaborate with just any association whatever calling itself religious, with the purpose of making common front against irreligion. . . . Certain manifestations of contemporary secularism, from the Biblical viewpoint, mark a spiritual progress rather than a regression. A common front of religions against irreligion would only result in an increase in present-day confusion. Such a course would reinforce the impression that there is a religion subjacent to those which already exist." [32]

Beneath the practical attitude of Catholicism rests the idea that the Biblical revelation comes, as a special case, from the common trunk which would be the natural religion of humanity. Of course, the Biblical revelation is the completion and fulfillment of this religion. Protestantism, denying this ontological tie, feels that in order to defend such and such human cause it can much more lucidly ally itself with an entirely secularized movement rather than run the risk of a secret and dangerous syncretism by joining in a common front of monotheistic religions.

This quite different estimation of secularization, which is the sociological background of the Western world, obviously involves some different conceptions in what concerns the relationships between church and state. But ecclesiological divergences interfere with this estimation of secularization. To the degree that Catholicism considers the church not only as the people of God assembled by the power of the Holy Spirit, but even more as a hierarchical society mediating salvation, as an institution disposing and distributing the means of salvation, it obviously tends to overestimate the authority of the church, to conceive of the church as a spiritual power (the idea of the temporal power of the church has indeed been abandoned). Being a power, the church must define its relations with other powers, in particular with the state. Persuaded that the temporal power of the state and its own spiritual power are two indissolubly linked aspects that go together for the good and happiness of man, the Catholic Church will have a tendency to call whenever possible for an official place in the state. It will lay claim to having officially its word in the elaboration of juridical rules concerning marriage, the family, and in the organization of the educational system. (In 1967, when the State of Württemberg abolished the confessional status of schools, the ecclesiastical authorities raised a vigorous protest and considered bringing action against the state for violation of the constitution.) In the encyclical *Immortale Dei* of November 1, 1885, Pope Leo XIII quite clearly formulated the doctrine of the church in this matter: "Nevertheless, their authority (that of the church and that of the state) is exercised over the same subjects, and therefore it can sometimes be the case that one and the same thing can, under different headings, be subject to the jurisdiction of both powers. . . . Therefore it is necessary for there to be a full harmony between the two powers, which one can rightly compare to the union that exists in man between the soul and the body." Of course, this text is older, but it has never been repudiated. According to the circumstances, favorable or unfavorable, the Catholic Church will seek to obtain a more or less complete harmony. Although since the Second Vatican Council the doctrine of thesis and hypothesis has largely been abandoned to determine the part of religious liberty that it is necessary to grant to non-Catholics, this doctrine still determines the attitude of the Catholic Church in regard to the different states.

We should not misappreciate what is valid in this attitude, which arises from the rejection of a too snug distinction between the spiritual and the temporal. The analysis of the Catholic Church is correct in the sense that the state could not be a simple technical authority. Its most technical decisions involve moral values. Despite its nonconfessionalism, it can never entrench itself in a moral neutrality, and that is precisely why the churches will be quite affected by the state's decisions, which will interfere with their own teaching. As Charles Journet writes: "The distinction between temporal and spiritual would be easy if . . . one had to understand by temporal that which is material and visible, and by spiritual that which is immaterial and invisible. . . . On the contrary, it is certain that the state must concern itself with human and moral values which are not visible. On the other hand, it is no less certain that the church of Christ is not invisible; it is in the likeness of Christ, that is to say, incarnate in material realities." [33]

The church is not wrong in rejecting this dichotomy which would turn it into a purely marginal and ineffective reality in relation to social development. The whole question is of knowing, as indeed a good number of Protestant churches are faced with knowing, whether it is right, in order to fulfill its function in the civil society, for the church to want to seek a privileged situation in the state, for it to want to be granted an authoritative status. For from the time that the church as organization sees this status granted it, an ambiguity will appear in the very nature of the church and in its authority. It will appear that this authority is conferred on it by the civil society, whereas this authority should have no other source but the Word of God. One perhaps will claim that this authority is not conferred but only recognized by the civil society. But where would the civil society obtain this spiritual lucidity? Barth justly asserts that "the civil community is spiritually blind and ignorant." [34] Misunderstanding is always near when we see the civil authority bending before the ecclesiastical power, for either the civil authority will consider the ecclesiastical power to be a political force which it is prudent to respect, or it will view it as a form of the sacred, that is to say, of that non-Christian and perhaps anti-Christian religious category from which secularism has only tenuously freed us. And by accepting or by claiming an official power in society, the church only witnesses to the fact that it does not itself believe that which is the source of its true authority, the Word.

It is not that the church should enclose itself within a pietism and give up exercising an action on the social and even political evolution. It is too ready to do this, too tempted to confine itself within the religious margin of life that secularization has left for it. But why would it be wrong to thus confine itself? Georges Crespy gives a pertinent reply to this question: "Like it or not, the church must enter politics because that is where there are men whom God loves. Of course, they are elsewhere. In fact, they are essentially elsewhere, since through the resurrection of Christ they are in the world visited by light. But they are elsewhere by remaining there, that is, they are simultaneously elsewhere and there. And although the church gives evidence of the elsewhere, it can do so only by being there. There is no elsewhere that does not pass by the there, as there is nothing of God that does not pass, or rather whose knowledge does not pass, by the man Jesus." [35] Since it is in the world of politics, in the broadest sense of the word, that man lives the greatest part of his existence, since it is in that world that we encounter his principal ethical problems, his temptations, and his sufferings, and that he is exposed to the primary dangers menacing his humanity, it is unthinkable that the church would not be with him there and would not attempt to take in hand the dangers to which he is exposed. That means, of course, an intervention of the church in the political and social life. But the whole question is one of knowing how the church should intervene. If it intervenes as an official power, it will become tied up with the political power or else will be in opposition to the political power. Thus the real motives of its intervention will be obscured. It will make common cause with a certain order of the world and will no longer

78

be devoted to its transformation (Rom. 12:2). Its intervention will lose the quality and meaning of witness. Therefore, it is necessary for the church to have recourse only to means that will not disqualify it as church. It can act only by persuasion, education, example, that is, by means which are only extensions of its preaching. Even when the church protests or participates in movements of protest, it is necessary that this protest be clearly tied to the prophetic element of its preaching, that is to say, that it be a sign of the announcement of the renewal of all things.

In sum, that which frequently opposes Catholic ethics and Protestant ethics on this point is that Catholic ethics refuses to see the chance that secularization offers to the action of the church. It also rejects the idea that the world of politics is a fully secularized world. It would like that world to preserve religious structures on which the church could take support. Protestant ethics, on the other hand, at least in intention if not always in fact, accepts the analysis that the political sphere is secularized, so that the church can freely defend and manifest the values to which it is attached due to the Word of God, these values which can be signs of the Kingdom of God. If the Protestant Church feels ill at ease in a communist state, it is essentially because such a state is not spiritually neutral, because it professes an official and constraining ideology, because it is not more secularized than a clerical state.

There is another question, one that seems decisive in the eyes of the Catholic Church. Even if it loses all official privilege, will its right at least be preserved in the collective society? Will there be a legal statute passed which will recognize its nature as a public establishment of international law? Catholic ethics and Protestant ethics can unite on this obviously different type of question. In defending its right to existence and to freedom, its right not only to preach and to evangelize publicly but also to have an external action conform to this preaching, a Christian church fights at the same time for the recognition of the right of

79

all human communities. It does not claim a special privilege in the name of a special prestige which the sacred should enjoy in any society. It asks for the recognition of a right of association which is part of all human existence. It protests against all legislation of exception and at the same time it takes the defense of all minorities. The only difference that could be brought up here between Catholic ethics and Protestant ethics is one of emphasis. In the eyes of the Catholic Church, this legally guaranteed and assured liberty is a primary and absolute condition. At the extreme, many Protestant churches would be tempted to think that this liberty can always be taken by a faithful church when it is refused by the public powers. With some temerity, but not completely without reason, Karl Barth replied in these terms to a pastor of the German Democratic Republic who had asked him if the church should not defend itself against a state that restrains its freedom: "A church that would have the obligation or at least the permission to take its own defense? I no longer believe in its claim to a sort of public right. Certainly, the church has a perfect right to hope that the state and society will enable it to freely proclaim its message. If this is granted, then the church will avail itself of the opportunity with gratitude. But this is not a right, and it is nonsense to boast of it. . . . Do you not think that to the degree in which you and we are truly the bearers of this good news—but who would dare to affirm otherwise?—the good news will have in itself sufficient vigor to make its place where its former zones of activity would have been suppressed or painfully contracted? Such a place that one fine morning its oppressors will be astounded!" [36]

There certainly is temerity in this proposal, for the church could not forget that wherever its freedom is restricted, other groups and other people will suffer the same violence, no matter how deeply the church remains the friend of the poor. Yet we should not forget either that the church must also bear in mind that its own freedom, in the

80

final analysis, has a foundation other than that of civil legislation.

4. Soul and Body;
Virtue and Perfection;
The Sexual Life

The most obvious differences between Catholic ethics and Protestant ethics are located on the level of problems concerning the social life. Yet we know, from our reflections on the relations of nature and supernature, that differences also exist, in a more subtle fashion, on the anthropological level, and that they bring about important cleavages in the domain of personal ethics.

Catholic thought, being strongly influenced by Greek ethics and in particular by the ethics of Aristotle, has never completely freed itself from the Greek dualism of body and soul. This dualism does not coincide with that of nature and supernature, for the soul is a part of nature just as the body is. But there are some points of convergence between the two dualisms, for the fine point of the soul is the receptacle of the supernatural.

According to traditional anthropology, the human being is not a simple nature. He is composed of body and soul, which have radically distinct properties. The soul is a simple and indecomposable substance, and consequently, following the perspective of Greek philosophy, the soul is not subject to death. In the *Dictionnaire de théologie catholique,* we read: "The soul of man is immaterial: it has neither quality nor extension; since matter is incapable of engendering it, it was created free and immortal by God; through the intelligence and the will, it communes with the eternal and the absolute, although by its vegetative and sensitive powers it is rivetted to the material." [37] The Christianization of the Greek idea of the soul has consisted essentially in the introduction of the idea of creation, by

81

which a certain contingency is introduced. The soul does not exist for all eternity; it has a beginning. Its existence depends on the contingent act of creation. The properties that the soul possessed in and of itself in the Greek perspective, namely, freedom and immortality, are still conserved by the soul by reason of its simplicity, but it owes them to the creative act of God. But God is creator of the substance soul, and the properties of this substance belong to it in an irrevocable fashion: simplicity and immateriality are the inamissible attributes of the soul. The fathers of the church hesitated simply on the question of knowing if immortality should also be considered as one of these attributes of the soul. Certain fathers thought that the soul had only an extrinsic immortality, that is to say, superadded by a special gift of the Creator and not a corollary of the nature of the soul. Plato, on the other hand, tried to deduce immortality beginning with the simplicity of the soul (*Phaedrus*). To be sure, such a conception does not find many Scriptural supports, for in Scripture it is not clear that the soul possesses any privileges over the body. It is the totality of being that depends on the free creation, on the free grace of God. Man appears in Scripture as a radically contingent being. The author of the article just quoted readily recognizes that the Thomist doctrine of the soul is not found explicitly in the Scripture, but he explains it by the fact that Scripture is not a metaphysical treatise. And he adds: "Moreover, although the concept of the spirituality of the human soul is encountered nowhere in Scripture with that preciseness which even the fathers themselves did not know how to give it and which Saint Thomas was able to give it, one still finds numerous and sufficiently clear passages in Scripture that favor the immateriality of the soul and its superiority over the body." [38]

J. Bainvel, who edited the Biblical article in the above-mentioned work, concludes it in these terms: "In short, the Bible clearly indicates the distinction of soul and body and the superiority of man over animal; the spirituality of

82

the soul is everywhere implied there; its unity and the identity of the principle, of the thinking principle, disengages sufficiently from the vital principle, despite certain texts that could raise some difficulties." [39] At no time does the author ask himself if perhaps in his reading of the texts he has applied a grid that is foreign to the Biblical anthropology and spirituality. That man is created in the image of God does indeed imply a distinction and a superiority of man in relation to the ensemble of the visible creation. But the Bible always speaks to us of man in his total existence, not as a composite. He is not the image of God only in his soul, by the vital breath that God puts in him as in all living beings. He is the image of God in all his being. Of course, Catholic thought certainly intends to respect this unity of the human being, but it does so by means of the Greek idea that only the soul gives the body its form, as the Demiurge gives a form to the primeval chaos of matter by making it an organized whole, a harmonious cosmos.

To quote Peillaube: "The self is one and the same. It is divided into two substantial principles: a principle of extension, which is the body, and a principle of activity represented by the soul. In its organic life it is simple and immanent, endowed with consciousness and sensible appetites in its sensitive life, and in the intellective life it is raised to such a degree of simplicity that it breaks its corporal bonds, and is constituted intrinsically independent, with its own life and laws, despite a certain extrinsic dependence in regard to the senses. Now, the substance of the soul must be defined by those of its functions which characterize it. The human soul is distinguished from other souls by intelligence and will, which are spiritual faculties. The substance of the soul is therefore a spiritual substance. Insofar as certain of these functions depend intrinsically on the body, it is the form of the body; insofar as it possesses functions intrinsically independent of the body, it is a subsisting form. Under this latter reference, the substance

83

of the soul is self-sufficient to exist and act. As form of the body, it gives to the body what it is capable of receiving: being, life, sensibility. Although the essence of the body is distinguished from that of the soul, it has no other existence than that of the soul. The human compound is thus a complex and unique whole, having only one sole existence, one sole being, one sole substance. It is the Aristotelian monism." [40]

We began by speaking of a dualism inherent in Catholic anthropology. Here it is a question of a monism. But we must understand that this monism concerns only personal existence and poorly overcomes a basic dualism of essences.

This doctrine has an incidence on the way in which man's destiny is conceived. Peillaube indicates this in the following way: "Man is composed of two distinct and irreducible substances, body and soul. The body returns to dust while awaiting the resurrection; the soul returns to God. Its principle is to unite once again with the resuscitated body. Such are the givens of the faith." [41] Such is, in any case, the meaning that Catholicism gives to the resurrection of the body. In fact, the resurrection concerns only the body. The immortal soul, by its essence, lives in eternity before being once again united with the resuscitated body. And yet, since the soul is not unscathed by sin, it has need of a pedagogical purification. The doctrine of purgatory thus has its roots in this astonishing anthropology.

It is astonishing because it introduces a distinction between essence and existence, for which it would be difficult to find Scriptural roots. The unity of existence is accompanied by a duality of essence, and since in Scholastic thought essence has more worth than existence, the duality of essence destroys the unity of existence.

It is through this schema of distinct essences that Catholic theology understands the New Testament ideas of *sarx*, *sōma, psychē,* and *nous.* Catholic theology does not seem to have understood that these terms designate not substantial

84

parts of the human person, but aspects of the person, manners of being of the entire person, and these are relative to the history which man lives in his relationship with God. These terms describe man's historical situations. As Mehl-Koehnlein has pointed out: "The anthropological ideas employed by the apostle Paul always refer to an indivisible totality. Human reality does not come down to a certain nature, whose parts one could distinguish and then study the manifestations corresponding to these parts. The soul and the body are not constituent and separable elements of one and the same 'I.' The body, the intellect, the flesh do not designate parts of man, but each time the entire man in certain manifestations of himself." [42]

Moreover, as the same author notes, these ideas have an immediate ethical significance. "The entire man," in his physical reality as well as in his psychical and spiritual reality, becomes *sarkikos,* when he turns aside from God, just as he becomes *pneumatikos* when he is justified by grace. One is in danger of missing the way from anthropology to ethics if this ethical and consequently historical orientation is not seen (historical, because the ethical qualifications of man appear in a history, the history of man's relationship with God and his neighbor). One would have a great deal of difficulty asserting the global and radical nature of sin, as long as the soul is defined as a simple and spiritual substance and which, consequently, by rights should not be sinful. If the soul is sinful, it is because of its relationships with the body. So once again we find the scarcely Christianized Platonic assertion that the body is the tomb of the soul. How is this possible, when the body is called to be the temple of the Holy Spirit? In any case, the tendency then is to place sin on the side of the body and consequently to make the body the ethical obstacle par excellence. This is the rather strange interpretation given to the Pauline affirmation that "the spirit is willing, but the flesh is weak," as if the ethical life were a fight between two antagonistic principles, as if the soul were

85

not fully engaged in carnal temptation. Even though the influence of Biblical and exegetical renewal has begun to shake up this anthropology within Catholicism, one can read the following declaration by Father Häring, as he describes perfect communion among men: "This inclination to the spiritual identity of natures from person to person encounters *the obstacle of matter* here below . . . spirits in quest of communion must compromise here below with a 'lowly body' (Phil. 3:21), the weight of a flesh and a matter imperfectly submissive to the domination of the spirit. Finally, Christ comes, who conforms our body to his glorious body (*ibid.*), who makes it a 'spiritual body' (I Cor. 15:44). Then the material part of our being and the cosmos to which it ties us will serve in an ineffable way the intercommunion of spirits." [43] This passage contains an amazing mixture of truth and of error. The truth is that full communion will indeed be possible only when our body will be rendered in conformity with the body of Christ. The error is that this body is seen only under the material category, as if only the matter in us sets up opposition to the action of the Holy Spirit, as if the fact of having a body, of living an incarnate existence, represented a metaphysical misfortune for us.

The ethical consequences of this dualistic anthropology, of this anthropology that makes a division between the essence of two components of man and the existence of the person, are extremely varied.

Because the body is matter, because it is deprived of the simplicity and the spirituality of the soul, because it is promised another destiny than the soul, it does not have the same dignity. Catholic ethics is far from having integrated the analysis of the body as it is proposed by modern existentialism and preeminently by the Christian existentialism of a Catholic philosopher such as Gabriel Marcel. Marcel's analysis of the human condition discloses to us the fact that I cannot interpret my body as a simple instrument external to my person. I exist bodily, as person. The

86

body is not a bit of matter which is associated in contingent fashion with my destiny. It is my "own body," it is the "absolute mediator" in the world of intersubjectivity, in the world of interpersonal relationships. It is through it that I am exposed to others. It is by it that I am exposed to that event which reaches me in the depth of my being, death. That death reaches me through my body is precisely the sign of the intimacy of the body in relation to the person, the sign that the soul is not thrown into a body that is foreign to it, but that it has the reality of the incarnation as the basic reference point. We readily murmur as if the body were foreign to us. We say: If I had been born during another age, if I had had different parents, if I had been born larger or smaller, my whole destiny would have been different. In such talk, we postulate a sort of externality to us of all that concerns the body. We turn it into an ensemble of variable factors, and in doing so, we give a foothold to a materialistic determinism. Man is never so materialist as when he is alienated from his body and puts aside the body into an objective externality of which the person becomes either the product or the victim. It is at the moment when my body no longer is integrated with my person, when I pretend to think that it no longer is my body, when I remove it from the side of the "inventoriable" that I really pass under its domination. Dietrich Bonhoeffer had not read Marcel, but he had reflected on the givens of Biblical anthropology, and he presents us with a vision of the body and of bodily life that Catholic theology has not yet been able to accept. In his *Ethics*, Bonhoeffer writes: "The life of the body, like life in general, is both a means to an end and an end in itself. To regard the body exclusively as a means to an end is idealistic but not Christian. . . . It is from this point of view that the body is conceived as the prison from which the immortal soul is released forever by death. According to the Christian doctrine, the body possesses a higher dignity. Man is a bodily being, and remains so in eternity as well. Bodiliness and human life belong inseparably together. And thus the bodiliness which is willed by God to be the form of existence of man is entitled to be called an end in itself. This does not exclude the fact that the body at the same time continues to be subordinated to a higher purpose. But what is important is that as one of the rights of bodily life its preservation is not only a means to an end but also an end in itself." [44]

Since it sets out from a completely different anthropology, Catholic thought does not arrive at these same ethical conclusions. It is still not completely healed of a certain scorn of the body, which one can find traces of in important areas. Whatever be the various motivations that led the church at the beginning of the twelfth century to establish and then maintain the celibacy of priests, it is certain that this law implies the following idea: the religious life is the form par excellence of the Christian life, it is the Christian life in perfection. This is precisely why it must be tied to various forms of asceticism, which have the object of subduing the body, of limiting its power over the person. In particular, that eminent form of bodily life which is the sexual life must not find any place in the life of the priest. There seems to be a sort of incompatibility between the holy function par excellence, which is to offer God the Eucharistic sacrifice, and the sexual life. The sexual life seems to put man in a kind of state of impurity. Of course, this understanding of things is becoming increasingly contested. Yet, although the Council authorized the consecration of married deacons, it refused the same authorization for the priests. What can be the reason for this difference if not the fact that the deacon, although he can distribute the Eucharistic elements, cannot himself offer the sacrifice and proceed to the consecration of the elements?

It is certain that Catholic ethics has undertaken a vigorous attempt to give renewed value to the state of marriage and that it strenuously emphasizes the holiness which can be realized in and through marriage. Nevertheless, it is far from having completely abandoned the idea that the finality of marriage is twofold, and that there is a hierarchy between the two ends of marriage.[45] The first is the most important, and clearly prevails over the second. The first, of course, is procreation, and the second is the conjugal community. Both, to be sure, imply the sexual life. But what gives worth to the first end is that the sexual life is clearly subordinated to a goal, both social and religious, the goal of procreation, of the perpetuation of the species, which is part of God's plan. What saves the sexual life, what renders it legitimate, is its subordination to a goal that surpasses it. Thus we see the continuing hesitation of the church to recognize as legitimate the various forms of birth control, not only because some of them reputedly are not natural but because their use permits the dissociation of the sexual life from procreation. Now, the sexual life seems pardonable only to the degree that it is just a means to an end. There is probably no Catholic theologian who could subscribe to this bold assertion of Bonhoeffer: "If the body is rightly to be regarded as an end in itself, then there is a right to bodily joys, even though these are not necessarily subordinated to some higher purpose. It is inherent in the nature of joy itself that it is spoilt by any thought of purpose." [46]

It is quite possible that the secret legalism which so often appeared in Catholic moral thought has its source, like all legalism, in a dualism. Legalism triumphs in Kant precisely because his anthropology is fundamentally dualistic and because reason has the task of constraining the sensible nature. To the degree that the body is not essential to human nature in Catholicism, to that same degree it can only be treated with a certain suspicion. The fact that the body is called to die and that the soul does not die attests sufficiently to the essential unworthiness of the body.

Rudolf Schnackenburg,[47] a Catholic theologian who has drafted a purely Biblical ethic, has seen in regard to I Cor.

6:12-20 how much the body is intimately tied to the spiritual destiny of man, that the body is for the Lord, as the Lord is for the body, and that the promise of resurrection goes for the entire man. Schnackenburg also points out how the concern of Catholic ethics for the soul alone has resulted in a narrowing of the much vaster and cosmological perspectives of salvation in Christ: "It is to be regretted that this motif of the eschatological participation in the consummated Kingdom of God has been reduced to our present desire 'to go to heaven.' We thus blur the great cosmic vision in favor of the individual blessedness of each one after his death, and the Christian himself is tempted, moreover, to think more of the salvation of his personal soul than of the fulfillment of the history of salvation, more of his own happiness than of the glorification of God." [48]

Conforming to the perspective inherited from antiquity, which concentrates the moral life in the adventure of the soul, Catholic ethics, following Saint Thomas, has insisted a great deal on *virtue*. During the present time we are witnessing a revalorizing of this idea of virtue, which has been criticized because it was considered as a simple habit. In Pinckaers' words, "Repeated acts hollow out a deep and lasting groove in the soul which one calls a 'habitus' and which is a kind of habit." [49] Now, this definition of virtue is morally suspect, for if virtue is a habit, it certainly creates at the same time an automatism which diminishes the moral tone of the action and paralyzes the spirit of invention. Too often moral pedagogy is content with the acquisition of habits, where the montage of virtues is made under the control of a rigid moral law. The result is a strengthening of legalism. To quote Pinckaers again, "Because virtue is defined as the inclination to do actions conformed to the moral law and to avoid actions prohibited by that law, one imagines that one will be a virtuous man when one has created in oneself, through the repetition of good actions, all of the habits, all of the automatisms necessary in order

90

to act always in accord with the moral law." [50] Now, such would not be the definition of virtue in Saint Thomas, nor even in Aristotle: *"Virtus cujus libet rei determinatur in ultimum in quod res potest"* (Saint Thomas, I^a, II^{ac}, q. LV, a. 3). Thus virtue appears, Pinckaers tells us, "as the capacity which a power of action has to accomplish the maximum of what it is capable." Or again: "It is an active quality which disposes man to produce the maximum of which he is capable on the moral level, which gives his united reason and will the power of accomplishing the most perfect moral actions, actions the most elevated in human value." [51] And taking up the very formulas of Saint Thomas, Pinckaers concludes that virtue "makes good he who possesses it and renders his work good. Virtue permits man to do perfect moral work and to render himself perfect." Thus virtue enables man to realize in himself the resemblance of God the Creator, of whom he is the image. Of course, from the point of view of its acquisition, virtue is acquired through repetition, but through the repetition of good acts, of internal acts, and not simply of external measures. And these internal acts are shaped and proportioned by the reason and the will. Each repetition is therefore a victory of the intelligence and the will. Thus is explained the preservation of the inventive and creative nature of the moral life founded on virtue.

It would be difficult to find a Protestant ethic that would give such a place to virtue. Of course, Protestant ethics is not ignorant of the virtues. The apostle Paul integrated into the paraenetical part of his letters lists of virtues, often borrowed from popular Stoicism. But a Protestant ethic would retain the pedagogical significance of the virtues: it would see a useful measure in their acquisition, it would consider them as a stabilizing power. Or it would be more attentive to the reality designated or aimed at by the virtues. A good man is not only a man who reproduces with a certain facility and with a certain joy the comportments of goodness, even if he bends them a bit according to cir-

91

cumstances. He is a man who strains toward that inexhaustible object of aspiration, toward that value which is goodness.

In any case, a Protestant ethic would not assert that virtue renders good whoever possesses it and that it renders his work good. Virtue is either an adjunct of the moral life, or an object of aspiration: it is never the foundation of the moral life. It does not render man good. Here we are at the antipodes of Luther's thought, according to which a work is not good simply by its conformity to the moral law; it is good because it is accepted by God. That is to say, it is good because it proceeds from the heart of a man who is agreeable to God, of a righteous man, because he has been justified by God. The sinful man can have a thousand virtues. Yet he is not for that reason acceptable to God. The morality of virtues defines virtue as a certain optimum balance of the powers of the soul, a balance such that man can carry his natural qualities to their maximum effectiveness. But in defining virtue in this way, such a morality locates the moral life within that "nature" which, in the economy of sin itself, can be more or less fully realized but which does not render man righteous before God. The gospel reminds us that bad as we are, we can give good things to our children. The Catholic doctrine of virtues seems to forget this paradoxical situation and to bring about too deep a caesura between the ethical life and sanctification, which comes only from justification.

Because Catholic ethics is ordinarily an ethics of virtues, it does not consider sin in the same light that Protestant theology does. For Catholic thought, sin is the opposite of virtue. "The body," writes Bernard Häring, ". . . could not fall into dissoluteness if the spirit remains virtuous." [52]

Protestant thought, however, opposes sin to faith. Catholic thought readily insists on the plurality of sins. It introduces degrees of gravity among sins. Mortal sins can deprive us of salvation; venial sins certainly offend divine mercy, but they cannot deprive us of acquired salvation.

Protestant thought speaks more readily of sin in the singular. It encloses all sins in the radical sin of unbelief. It emphasizes that the disobedience of the first man originated in incredulity: "Hath God said?" Man begins on the road of disobedience through doubt in the Word of God. So only faith and not primarily the practice of virtues can heal us from sin. Whatever be its form, whatever be its gravity in regard to the neighbor, whatever be the degree of failing in regard to the commandments of God, sin always has the same nature: it is a refusal to believe that the word of God is good, righteous, true. Of course, pedagogical reasons normally and legitimately can bring about the outlining of a hierarchy of sins. The proper appraisal of responsibility not only on the juridical level but also on the ethical level can even require such a hierarchy. The Christian, knowing that all men are sinners, should not console himself too easily, should not absolve himself, or take lightly such sin under the fallacious pretext that "at night all cats are gray" and consequently one should not be too concerned over the degree of sin. Indeed, the apostle reminds us that certain forms of sin are incompatible with entrance into the Kingdom of God: "For be very sure of this: no one given to fornication or indecency, or the greed which makes an idol of gain, has any share in the kingdom of Christ and of God" (Eph. 5:5, NEB; cf. Gal. 5:21). However, note that these serious sins are put into relationship with idolatry, that is to say, with unbelief. But reciprocally, those who do not commit these abominations must not imagine that the absence of these scandalous sins can signify righteousness and that they are therefore forgiven. As the confession of sins of Ch. Bahut says: "We confess, Lord, that our common end, honest sinners or shameful sinners, would be despair and perdition." All sin attests our separation from God, all sin is connected with radical sin, which is the refusal to believe.

If Catholic ethics so readily gives preeminence to the virtue of temperance and the asceticism that this virtue implies, is it not ultimately because it believes in the possibility of a healing of sinful man by means of psychoethical techniques? According to Häring: "Man marked by original sin can neither acquire nor keep temperance without an asceticism, that is to say, without an assiduous observation of the self and a liberal amount of work on the self. The internal disorder of sinful man is so great that the virtue of temperance not only requires a general asceticism, a methodical discipline, but even more, a self-abnegation and a habitual renunciation even of the pleasures that remain compatible with temperance. *In order to keep his equilibrium in the serenity of the righteous milieu, the son of Adam, carried along by sensuality, has need of willingly breaking with the permitted usage of worldly things, even with the legitimate enjoyment of sensual activity.*" [53]

Certainly no fault can be found with the idea of a discipline, and the preaching of Christian freedom must always be balanced by the call to a necessary discipline. But does not the overemphasis on this discipline entail the danger of leading to believe that it can uproot sin? Does it not risk giving rise to that form of pride which is born from the domination that man—precisely sinful man—is quite capable of exercising over himself? Undoubtedly, the author of these lines can assert that he is addressing the baptized, who believe that their sin has already been swallowed up in the death of Christ and that consequently it is only a matter of an inner discipline of the life in faith. But he nevertheless leaves the great faith-sin opposition blurred, which is the key to the mystery of the ethical life. The liberation from sin through faith must result in putting ascetic and disciplinary practices on a secondary rank. They should not be scorned, but used pedagogically. And it is necessary to remember that the transposition of pedagogical precepts into rules of faith ordinarily is heretical. In the apostle's words: "Did you not die with Christ and pass beyond reach of the elemental spirits of the world? Then why behave as though you were still living the life of the

94

world? Why let people dictate to you: 'Do not handle this, do not taste that, do not touch the other'? . . . That is to follow merely human injunctions and teaching. True, it has an air of wisdom, with its forced piety, its self-mortification, and its severity to the body; but it is of no use at all in combating sensuality" (Col. 2:20-23) .

The Catholic insistence on sins, on the hierarchy of sins, parallels the insistence on virtues. The two attitudes result in bringing about a sort of dissociation between the event of faith and the ethical life. Of course, this dissociation is not desired, but the link between justification and sanctification is not maintained strictly enough. Because sins are not seen as the manifestation of the one sin of incredulity, ethical healing is not clearly sought in justification itself, but in the virtues. And one questions oneself to discover what sins can make us lose the benefit of salvation, whereas only unbelief, the refusal of grace, can exclude us from that which God has accomplished once for all.

But perhaps the opposition goes even farther. It bears on the nature and consequently on the gravity of sin itself. Catholic tradition speaks of sin as a wounding of human nature, and on occasion, as with Father Häring, as an unruliness and a disorder. Here we come again across the distinction between nature and supernature. Sin has cut nature off from its supernatural extension and in the very bosom of nature it produces disorder and unruliness.

Catholic theology has often maintained that the act of sin could not be entirely bad. This is not because Catholic theology has accepted the ancient doctrine which says that evil is nothing but a privation, a lack, an absence. It has always asserted that this privation is accompanied by a positive malice—which means that no act done by a sinful man can be *formally* good. But it is not, from this fact, necessarily evil. The *Dictionnaire de théologie catholique* states: "Although, in the act of sin, there remains nothing of formal goodness, there does remain and will always remain something of fundamental goodness. This latter point can easily be established. In effect, there is no evil act whose constituent moral principles are completely corrupted, i.e., the object, end, and various circumstances. For such complete corruption to be present, there would have to be such an unlikely accident or such a clever cunning that the case would be chimerical. We concede that the event is not metaphysically impossible and that it is not absolutely inconceivable that a human act be encountered which is corrupted in all its parts. Yet there remains something else which saves our thesis. For in this act, there still remains its relationship with reason. We can say that the very fact of proceeding from reason, and with a regard to reason, constitutes a fundamental goodness that is indestructible. Moreover, the moral goodness of this act is founded on this relation to reason. Also, because of this relation, the act, object, circumstances, and end must be good, for from the fact that man acts as reasonable, the law of reason dictates that he act with a good object, etc., this is to say, with all the reasonable rectitude which the matter in which he is acting requires. . . . Thus, in every human act there at least subsists this fundamental goodness, which, in remaining, is variable in consideration of the basis of moral goodness, according as it is conjoined with a more or less great malice. And, as we have said that the privative malice of sin is immediately opposed to the fundamental goodness, one must confess that this privation cannot be absolute." [54]

Several things should be underlined in this text. For one thing, there is the assertion that the acts of sinful man are never fundamentally bad, from the sole fact that they conserve some relation with reason for the determination of their object, circumstances, and end. But even more important, there is the assertion that reason, which belongs to man's nature, preserves its rectitude in the economy of sin, that it in some way is exempt from the sinful history of humanity. It is also necessary to observe that the analysis of the Catholic theologian bears on the constitution and structure of the act, more than on the subject of the act. In the act, one seeks to isolate parts which would not in themselves be bad, which would even be good. A Protestant theologian, on the contrary, would bring the weight of his reflection to bear on the subject himself, would give little worth to this quantitative analysis, and would wonder if from the fact of sin it is not the very "heart" of man which is evil and unjust, even if the acts can have some moral efficacity, some social utility, or witness to certain qualities or virtues. In other words, the Protestant reflection on sin is disengaged from ethical concepts so that attention may be paid to the relationship of the subject with God. And since it discovers that this relationship, as Scripture testifies, is not a relationship of righteousness outside of faith, it concludes, without having to pronounce on the ethical value of individual acts, that such acts are not good. Only the man who is at peace with God can do acts that are acceptable to God, that is, that are good.

Since the Reformation, Protestant ethics has consistently taught, except during the ages of rationalism and of liberalism, that sin is a total corruption of human nature. Thus its vision of man is fundamentally pessimistic, and Catholicism has not ceased to reproach Protestantism for this. A Catholic spirit as open as Emmanuel Mounier could write: "The most central Catholic tradition, for its part, has always rejected that disastrous propensity (to empty the creature on behalf of the Creator) in retaining to the creature, even wounded by sin, some natural powers of autonomy and recovery, in maintaining relations of reciprocal generosity under the relations of authority and dependence." [55] In fact, humanism has always found a more certain support on the side of Catholicism than of Protestantism. In a study that does not at all minimize the seriousness of sin (and speaks of a "nature totally engulfed in sin"), Father Maydieu nevertheless maintains the idea that "human nature remains in its integrity with intelligence and will, which permit freedom." [56]

We must recognize that Protestant ethics finds itself

97

rather perplexed in this matter. This was seen in the great controversy between Luther and Erasmus on the question of free will. The two adversaries carried on a battle that could not have any outcome. Erasmus rejected the doctrine of total sin. He wanted a part of freedom to subsist in man. Luther saw very clearly that to make this concession would lead to Pelagianism, and would strike at the sovereign grace of God. But at the same time, he could not deny that sinful man is capable of intelligent choice and decision. Sinful man has become neither animal nor thing. The difficulty undoubtedly comes from the idea of the total corruption of human nature. This idea had already created difficulty on the dogmatic level. In effect, if sin has produced this total corruption of the nature created by God, it follows then that the devil has had the power to destroy the good creation of God, that the very power of God has been checked, which is not really admissible. In fact, Scripture does not know this idea of the total corruption of human nature. It speaks more readily of sin as a captivity. Sinful man is a slave to evil powers. But what is a slave? It is not a man who has lost his human faculties of reflection, decision, and choice. He is still capable of doing great things. The masters of antiquity knew this quite well when they entrusted their slaves with the responsibility of managing their domains. A slave is a man who no longer disposes of the freedom that is his own. He is put, with his intelligence and his freedom, under another's control. Luther, in the choice of the title of his work, had an intuition of this paradoxical situation: *De servo arbitrio*. This alliance of words signifies that although sinful man is capable of a free judgment (*arbitrium*), it is this free judgment which is put into slavery. Thus man can and must be called totally sinner, without this implying that he becomes a subhuman, an automaton. It is necessary to maintain two affirmations at one and the same time: man is a free being, humanity is characterized by free will; but this freedom is prisoner of sin.

98

Protestantism has reason to smell the scent of a lingering Pelagianism in Catholicism, but Catholicism has reason to oppose the traditional doctrine of the corruption of human nature with the fact that sinful man is capable of accomplishing great things, of constructing a science, of creating civilizations and cultures, and of living an ethical life.

It is sufficient for Protestantism to recall that all these authentic values have been "imprisoned" under the law of sin.

To say, as we have done, that the primary difficulties between Catholic ethics and Protestant ethics are located on the level of anthropology is not, for that reason, to relativize them, for every Christian anthropology is rooted in Christology. It is not possible to say what man is without a twofold reference to Adam and Christ. If one wants to overcome the oppositions between Catholic ethics and Protestant ethics, one must give some attention to the point of articulation between anthropology and Christology, which means that the solution is to be found in a common recovery of the Scriptural witness.

III

THE CONVERGENCES

It would be naïve to think that the strong divergences which we have emphasized must be resolved before we are able to outline the convergences. The march of the churches toward unity does not necessarily follow a logical pattern. Moreover, the motifs that can produce a convergence on the ethical plan can be extremely diverse. It is possible that modifications in the method of theological reflection can have an unexpected effect in the untying of previously unresolvable difficulties. It is also possible that the necessity of confronting a completely new ethical or social situation will lead the churches to rethink their traditional ethics. The evolution of theological thought is linked, in fact, not only to its thorough investigations, to its effort to secure its foundation by returning to the center of the apostolic kerygma, but also to the challenges which the modern world presents to the churches. If there currently is a sincere ecumenical dialogue possible, whereas not long ago one witnessed a simple confrontation of opposed doctrines, it is related to these two types of causes that we have mentioned. In a secularized world, in which Christianity tends to become more and more in the minority, in which philosophies are engaged in directions that break away from union with a metaphysic more or less colored by Christianity, in which an ethic is being formulated whose attachment to Christianity has ceased to be evident,

100

in such a world, the Christian confessions no longer can seek support, as they did so often in the course of their history, in a certain number of common values. They no longer can begin with a certain number of truths recognized by all. More than ever, they must find their own foundation. When Bonhoeffer tells us that the hour has come for Christianity to become religionless, he means primarily that Christianity must live on the basis of its own foundation. Bonhoeffer writes: "What is bothering me incessantly is the question what Christianity really is, or indeed who Christ really is, for us today. The time when people could be told everything by means of words, whether theological or pious, is over, and so is the time of inwardness and conscience—and that means the time of religion in general. . . . Our whole nineteen-hundred-year-old Christian preaching and theology rest on the 'religious a priori' of mankind. 'Christianity' has always been a form—perhaps the true form—of 'religion.' But if one day it becomes clear that this a priori does not exist at all, but was a historically conditioned and transient form of human self-expression—what does that mean for 'Christianity'?" And Bonhoeffer then gives precise expression to his questions: "The questions to be answered would surely be: What do a church, a community, a sermon, a liturgy, a Christian life, mean in a religionless world? How do we speak of God—without religion, i.e., without the temporally conditioned presuppositions of metaphysics, inwardness, and so on?" [1]

Even if the various Christian churches are somewhat frightened by this unprecedented language, they cannot ignore the problem which faces them: they no longer find themselves in a world that forms a preliminary given on which they can base their teaching. They must have the courage, and they must have it together, to stake their teaching and preaching on the only foundation that truly belongs to them, Jesus Christ. If natural law and natural morality are being called into question in Catholic thought

101

at the present time, is it not because the truths that they contained, which were understood without difficulty by preceding generations, are disappearing, are precisely no longer truths?

On the other hand, a civilization founded on technology is gradually developing, and with it are developing effective techniques that no longer concern just the world of things and the world of natural forces—they concern man himself, in his ethical behavior. And with this development, the traditional teaching of the church has less and less hold over man, who believes that he is sufficiently secure through the techniques of which he disposes. And it has less and less hold over a society that learns how to resolve all its problems without having need of the hypothesis of "God," without even having need of religion as it still had need of religion at the time of Karl Marx, to give a spiritual aroma to its enterprises. For a long time, Christianity was able to present itself as the moral guide of society. At least this was the case in the West. Today this guide is no longer listened to, and even more, it isn't even recognized as a guide. One tolerates it in proportion to its ineffectiveness. If the church wants to regain an audience and an authority, it can no longer content itself with dictating duties to men and societies. It must rediscover ways of a friendship with men. It must be of service to them. It must become the church, servant of men. In any case, is the church not the servant of its Lord, of whom we say, *Ecce homo*? This means that the church has to come up with an ethic which is of service to the men of our time. Christian ethics no longer finds any justification as law imposed on men, but as service rendered to men. This need explains why a parallel effort to view and explain ethics under the form of service is coming both from the side of the member churches of the World Council of Churches and from the side of the Roman Church.

The conjunction of these two causes, namely, the necessity for a theology resting on its own foundations and not

102

having recourse to other evidences than those which are its own, and the necessity of an ethics of service in present times, explains both the renewal of confessional ethics and their convergences.

1. Biblical Renewal
and Its Effects on Ethics

The Biblical renewal within Catholic exegesis, which was made possible by a greater freedom afforded to scholars (beginning with the encyclical *Divino Afflante Spiritu,* 1943) is far from having already had its effects on the level of the systematic disciplines. Although the problem of the relations between Scripture and tradition are far from being clarified in Catholic theology (and perhaps also in Protestant theology), Scripture has, in fact, played a considerable role in the debates of the Council, and in the redaction of various constitutions and declarations. But as Oscar Cullmann [2] emphasizes, this role is not unambiguous. Sometimes, as in the second chapter of the constitution *Lumen Gentium,* the thought finds its substance and its norms in Scripture; sometimes on the contrary, as in Chs. 3 and 4 of the same constitution, the Scripture that is often cited merely brings certain *dicta probantia* to the support of a thesis which, in itself, is foreign to Biblical perspectives. As far as ethics is concerned, one notices that during the past few decades Catholic theologians have produced two types of works. On the one hand, there are systematic treatises which, in general, are repetitions of the thought of Saint Thomas. In a sporadic way, Saint Thomas is shown to have been in basic accord with Scripture (among works of this type, we should mention: Odon Lottin, *Morale fondamentale* [Paris: Desclée et Cie., 1954]; S. Pinckaers, *Le Renouveau de la morale* [Paris: Casterman, 1964]). These works are a sort of rereading of Saint Thomas in the light of the Biblical as well as the scientific knowledge

103

of today. In the preface to Pinckaers' work, Father Chenu outlines the meaning of the enterprise by denouncing the theological ethics of eternal truths which comes, according to Chenu, from the "crypto-Scholastic ontologies of the seventeenth and eighteenth centuries," from an "essentialist conception of truth, according to which the times somehow infect the life of the spirit and the intelligence of things, including morals." He feels that today a better understanding both of the life of the spirit and of the divine economy establish together, in the same fabric of truth, both the divine and the human, the delicate conjunction of history and the Spirit.[3]

The critique of the past and the new intention appear very clearly: according to Father Chenu, it is necessary to give up the idea of deducing ethics from some eternal verities, from an ontological metaphysic, in order to root it in a knowledge of man as historical being and in a knowledge of divine revelation which also is history.

Alongside these works of systematic ethics there is the novelty—for Catholicism—of numerous studies of Biblical ethics. Among the better efforts, we should mention the work of R. Schnackenburg, *Le Message moral du Nouveau Testament,* and the monumental study of Father C. Spicq, *Théologie morale du Nouveau Testament.* There is a relationship between these two series of works. To the degree that Catholic theology is moving away from an intemporal systematization, and of course from the legalism which is inherent in all such systematization, it tends to turn more directly toward Scripture, and in particular, toward the New Testament. As Spicq puts it: "Neither the Lord nor the apostles elaborated a complete and coherent moral system. Like the ancients, they were not concerned to give universal definitions, to analyze concepts, to deduce consequences starting with adequately formulated principles. Most often they were led to determine the conduct of the disciples on the basis of particular cases, of given persons, of such and such accidental and ephemeral conjunctures. And it is not easy to judge if this is a question of a 'situation ethic' or if the announced rule remains valid beyond the very concrete occasion that gave rise to it." [4] Spicq's observation is entirely correct: if the Gospels bring us an ethical teaching, it is always situated in an encounter of Jesus with some individual person. If, in the apostolic letters, the ethical teaching seems more systematized, it nevertheless is addressed to an individual community or to a precise person. Of course, all these indications are located within the vector of love. But love, precisely, cannot be transformed into a law, for the object of love is a very concrete neighbor. Only its exigence is universal; the forms in which it will express itself will vary infinitely. The very spontaneity of the ethical life of a justified and pardoned man is incompatible with a rational system of preestablished and codified precepts. It is necessary even to give up trying to transplant a given ethical imperative to our time and to seek to apply it mechanically. R. Schnackenburg ends his book with the following remarks: "Our Christian generation seems to be opening up the primitive Biblical Word once again. It sees it in the purity of the source and the power of the beginning. Thus it must also preach it without weakening it, that is to say, in the moral realm, to locate the exigences of the ethics of Jesus in our time in their wholeness and to apply them to ourselves. It is also to say that we do not need to chain ourselves tightly to the word and teachings which the writers of the New Testament meant for their own times. It is our job to engage for our times in the task that they accomplished then for their churches: to announce the message of Jesus with the same ardor of faith, with the same ethical seriousness, and with the same eschatological vigilance." [5]

What is the meaning of the coexistence in Catholicism of these two currents, of these two traditions, the one more metaphysical and related essentially to the structures of Thomist thought, the other more based on Biblical theology? For both currents are held to be valid. Of course, it is

105

perfectly legitimate to want to go beyond the level of Biblical theology in order to attempt a systematization, that is
to say, to discover beyond the manifold pattern and di-
versity of the Biblical witnesses a revelation as a whole
which is organized around a center. No theology could
avoid this need. But where is the principle of systematization to be found in an ontology of Thomist type? With
notable exceptions (Tillich and Thielicke, for example),
Protestant ethics attempts to start out from the Christological center and adopts this affirmation of Bonhoeffer: "The
point of departure for Christian ethics is not the reality of
one's own self, or the reality of the world; nor is it the reality of standards and values. It is the reality of God as He re-
veals Himself in Jesus Christ." [6] Catholic ethics, on the
other hand, skips back and forth between two different orientations; Thomism is normative, Scripture also. We propose the following interpretation: the Catholic Church
hesitates to abandon completely an ethic that takes its departure in universal affirmations, in a certain number of
principles possessing a rational evidentness and capable of
being attached to an ontology. Consequently, it hesitates
to turn its back on legalism. But this is because it dreads
falling into a situational ethic, even when such an ethic
would not make the concrete and historical situation the
only source of every ethical exigence, even when such an
ethic would see the situation only as the occasion offered
to the freedom of justified man to come up with a solution.
For such a hypothesis would destroy the ecclesiastical
magisterium, insofar as it has the power to dictate com-
portment to consciences through universal rules.

Now, an entirely Biblical ethics obviously calls for this
risk to be run, since the personal encounter with Christ
prevails over all principles, since justified and forgiven
man rediscovers a full liberty. This freedom which is not
a property of man but a gift of God is what Karl Barth has
founded his entire concrete ethic on (*Dogmatik* III/4).
Not that this freedom wipes away the commandment, the

will of God; the act of obedience, accomplished in faith, must itself be free. It ceases to be free if it is only determined by the imperative magisterium of the church. It is true that the magisterium addresses itself to believers, but the latter are expected to give carte blanche to the church. Their freedom is only potential. It is somehow suspended by the commandment of the church, which as social institution could do nothing but make rules and impose them with authority. Now, Paul says, "Christ set us free, to be free men" (Gal. 5:1).

Of course, no equivocation is possible: this freedom of the justified man has nothing to do with the arbitrary disposition of ourselves. It is a freedom that makes us free for obedience and service. But this obedience is always obedience to the one who has set us free from all that hinders us from being in the service of the brother. It is not obedience to norms that are established in necessarily juridical fashion by the ecclesiastical institution. The latter, in its preaching, must call us to freedom before everything else. Naturally, it must also instruct us and enlighten us regarding the concrete service that we can render today. It can do this with strength and authority to the degree that it has first called us to freedom. It can also subject us to a certain discipline, provided that it remembers itself that this discipline has a relative nature and that it concerns primarily the old man in us, which does not want to give its right place to the new man, to the free man. Discipline cannot go beyond the limits of pedagogical action without killing freedom and responsibility.

A present-day example will illustrate what we are trying to say: a new historical situation has been created by the scientific discoveries that permit man and woman to assume their parenthood differently than in the past. They can now make procreation a voluntary, reflective, and responsible act, more so than in the past. But in the face of this new situation, the Catholic Church has long hesitated to lift the very strict instructions that it had imposed on

107

its members.[7] These delays have an explanation, for the Catholic Church knows full well that in the present situation it cannot ultimately do otherwise than to say: Behave like responsible people; if you have serious reasons for wanting to space births, do it. Now, this is precisely what the Catholic Church does not want to say; it would much rather continue to give rules. Undoubtedly, freedom is dangerous, even for the Christian. That must be recognized. But it is spiritually even more dangerous not to run the risk of freedom. Of course, it belongs to Christian preaching to recall the limits of freedom. As Barth says, because this freedom is the gift of him who is our Creator and our Lord, it is called to be exercised within the limits which our Creator and Lord has outlined for us in his love: "The man limited by God is the object of his love. To be limited is the same thing as saying 'to be loved.' We have every right not simply to lament, but to take seriously, to accept and approve, from our side the fact that God has limited us in such a way that we be what we are, and nothing other—and to praise God for this great favor." [8] But the error—and it does not only menace the Catholic Church—is to first place limitations, to set up principles and rules, before having proclaimed man's liberation to him. The error is to fail to show man his limits starting from his freedom. The apostle Paul never ceases to proclaim himself as the *doulos* of the Lord, but this affirmation has meaning only within the good news of freedom.

Thus the persistence in Catholic ethics of two types of approach, the fact that it teaches simultaneously an ethic of principles and an evangelical ethic, is evidence of a sort of hesitation to give freedom its true place in the Christian life. Of course, the Catholic Church does not ignore or scorn freedom. But it does have a tendency to set up the ethical problem under the framework of a law and, consequently, of a power of the church, which decrees general principles or, by virtue of its pastoral magisterium, forbids

108

certain acts (joining a given political party, or a given secret society, etc.) . It is then that it asks the question of the margin of freedom which belongs, in the decision, to the Christian conscience. Karl Rahner, after having recalled the limits which the church places on the temporal activity of Christians, then and only then goes on to make appeal to the responsibility of the Christian: "The Christian is certainly expected to respect the general principles of the church, but he is no less expected *to search his own conscience,* and pursuant to the personal problematic before which he is placed as individual, the concrete imperative will permit him to fashion his own life and to bring his own building block to the edifice of public life." [9]

The approach proper to Catholic ethics consists thus in first setting up a general system of rules and then preparing a place within this system for the freedom of the faithful. This is why it hesitates to abandon the frameworks of its traditional systematization. The churches of the Reformation, for their part, do not abstain from giving their faithful certain general directives. But at least in principle these directives find their origin in a reflection on the gospel of grace and of the Kingdom. Therefore, they try not to stifle freedom, but to put the faithful in the presence of the requirements of this freedom.

The fact that the Catholic ethic, despite its systematic spirit, makes an increasingly large place for the Biblical message, indeed indicates that a profound *rapprochement* is under way between Catholic ethics and Protestant ethics. It does not suppress all the difficulties, for it would be naïve to think that Catholics and Protestants receive the Scripture without any preconceptions.

The hermeneutical problem is placed on the level of ethics as well as on that of dogmatics. One does not read Scripture without a certain interpretational procedure. It is true that currently the Biblicists of both confessions are faced with the same difficulties regarding the hermeneutical problem. And this problem undoubtedly will not be resolved soon. But the fact that Catholic theology, once it has gone beyond exegetical research and begins to work on dogmatic and ethical questions, must take account of the indications of the magisterium, itself the interpreter of a tradition, necessarily diminishes its freedom. This weight of the normative tradition is made felt even in the research of Biblical ethics. At the end of his great inquiry on the moral theology of the New Testament, Father Spicq sums up "the major aspects of New Testament ethics." He emphasizes correctly the unity of this ethics, but this unity seems to him to be essentially in the fact that it is an "ethic of authority" and that its first principle is "unquestioning consent" to religious subjection.[10] He is undoubtedly correct in emphasizing that the subject of the moral exigence is the sovereign Lord, before whom we are servants, but are the terms that he uses really adequate? Would not Protestant ethics be right in calling for more dialectical formulas, in the measure that this servant is also called by the Lord to a life of personal partnership in the bosom of a covenant, in the measure that he has not been made for the law, but the law has been made for him?

Spicq goes on to show that the moral teaching of the New Testament is a "religious morality," by which he means that it is a morality of holiness and perfection. But the question is precisely one of knowing if a religious morality, in the normal sense of the word, i.e., a morality whose imperatives take their authority from the sacred, that sacred which inspires fear in us, if such a morality can be a morality of holiness, that is, a morality founded on participation in faith, in the holiness of God. Of course, one could say that this is just a quarrel with words, that the author is following the Catholic tradition and employs the adjective "religious" for "Christian." But what is striking is that he does not characterize Christian morality as a morality of grace except in the third place. But is that not its primary and fundamental character? It is true that Spicq shows a great fidelity to the New Testament in-

110

spiration in his development, and that he cuts the ground
out from under any chance of legalism when he writes:
"But from the day that Christ brought 'the gift of God' to
men, morality no longer could be obedience to precepts,
but the correct and whole unfolding of a life." [11] He speaks
excellently of the growth of the inner man, of the dynamism of the new being born at baptism. And he emphasizes
that the true moral problem, since according to Gal. 2:20,
Christ lives in me, is "to allow the Lord to unfold his life
more and more sovereignly in our souls." [12] It would be
easy to find formulas of the same type in Barth and Bonhoeffer. Bonhoeffer, indeed, insists strongly on the fact that
the whole ethical becoming of man consists in allowing
Christ to take form in us, to be unceasingly conformed to
his image.[13] Spicq writes in the same fashion: "The Christian life is Christ continuing to live personally and morally in his own." [14] He also clearly insists on the eschatological dimension of the moral life and consequently on
the role of hope nourished and maintained in the heart
of the faithful by the Holy Spirit. A true Christian ethic
consists less in prescribing behavior for the different life
situations than in *saying* what has come for man and in
proclaiming the radical transformation of our lives by the
irruption of grace. It is the announcement of both a fact
and a promise. The only imperative that it can give us is:
Become really and concretely what you have already become in Christ, that is to say, that new man who, being acceptable to God, loves the righteousness of God. When it
is in conformity to the New Testament message, ethics
gives up enclosing human life in preestablished norms
and no longer substitutes constraint for the promise. When
it takes support on the reality of the new man, the convergence between Catholic ethics and Protestant ethics is
realized without difficulty.

Yet divergences reappear in the midst of this convergence, and they come precisely from the different reading
that we make of the same texts. Speaking of the new man

111

described in II Cor. 5:17 and Eph. 4:24, Spicq tells us that Christian morality is articulated on "an ontology" that the creature who yesterday was still a sinner "possesses in himself the foundation of his morality," [15] and that believers possess the same nature as God.[16] A little farther on he speaks of a "structure of being." [17] Or again, this rather astonishing phrase: "The neo-testamental virtuous can only be an exact reproduction of Jesus Christ." [18] Does one really speak of the reality of the new man, who is unceasingly recreated in us by the free gift of grace, in terms of ontology, structure, and possession? Do not these terms suggest the existence in us of a nature, undoubtedly created by God, but which acquires a sort of self-sufficiency or consistency of such a type that one can speak of it as of a possession?

Through this language we can understand one of the profound orientations of Catholic thought, which consists in an "objectivization" in man of that which God has accomplished for him. There is a subtle passage from the order of a gift to the order of a possession. Now, God does not withdraw his gift. His gift is his presence, and a presence could not become nature or structure. Grace is never possessed, but always received. Recourse to these ideas borrowed from an ontology or from a substantialist philosophy gets in the way of understanding that man never becomes that neotestamental virtuous person of whom Spicq speaks, that exact reproduction of Jesus Christ. For Christ takes form in man only so that he can stand erect before God and walk in the presence of God, that is, so that he can live in faith. Now, this faith is not a property of his nature. It, also, is a gift of God. And since it is not an inamissible attribute, the old man subsists and continues to make reappearances. Catholic thought, because it speaks a substantialist and ontological language, has never been able truly to appropriate the decisive truth for all ethical existence of Luther's formula: *"Semper justus ac peccator."* In other words, the ethics of the New Testament can be

112

interpreted only in terms of existence and not in terms of substance. We cannot define the being of the Christian man. We can only say what his existence is when he walks, in faith, before the Eternal. The great traditional debate between Catholics and Protestants on the persistence of the image of God in man is insoluble insofar as it is put in terms of being or of possession. Man becomes in Christ the image of God only in a believing existence.

Biblical renewal will not produce a complete convergence between Catholic ethics and Protestant ethics except in the measure that the two theologies move forward together toward the solution of the problem of Biblical hermeneutics.

2. *The Renewal of Social Ethics*

Biblical renewal undoubtedly is the profound and permanent source of the renewal of Christian ethics, of their actualization, of their liberation from moral systems imposed at a certain moment in history by dominant social classes.

The secondary source of their renewal is paradoxically this secularized, technical, industrial society which progressively extends its structures over the whole world, without its development being controlled by the churches. The Western world, more or less profoundly Christianized, and its civilization, which was diffused by colonialist enterprises, predominated and considered itself to be *the* civilization, and this led the churches to nourish the hope that in view of the universalization of this civilization, they could extend what they considered Christian morality to cover the whole inhabited world. This perspective is no longer possible today. The churches have become a minority and have to assume the nature of a diaspora. And confronting the churches is a secular Catholicity, based on this

113

new technical civilization, a Catholicity foreign to Christian Catholicity. It would be a great temptation for the churches, in these conditions, to begin a movement of withdrawal, which secularizing forces suggest to them and sometimes try to impose on them. But this is not the course that they are presently taking. On the contrary, we are witnessing quite a different thing, both from the side of the World Council of Churches, and more recently, from the side of the Catholic Church. There is a serious attempt to face the new ethical problems posed by this secular Catholicity and to propose a certain number of ethical approaches, approaches which the Christian faith justifies but which can have a meaning and value for all men. This is the source of the remarkable proliferation today of works of social ethics in Christianity. It is also the source of the effort of the churches to confide less responsibility for carrying out a Christian ethic in the hands of their leaders and to encourage laymen to be present in all of the enterprises of the human adventure. (This new orientation is expressed by the overabundant use in ecclesiastical language of the term "engagement," or "involvement".) Laymen are asked to live fully with non-Christians in all the attempts made to permit a growing economy, a cultural and social development which gives man the possibility of fully expressing himself and of realizing all his possibilities.

Of course, this humanism is anything but Christian. But its realization and that of social justice can rightly be considered by the churches as signs of their hope, of the hope of the Kingdom. They will consider that it is worth the trouble to build on such signs, which attest the love of God for all creatures, which attest—of course, for faith—that in Jesus Christ, God has truly reconciled the world to himself and that he has pronounced the yes of his mercy on the creative activity of men, even when it is and remains marked by sin. There is an extremely important theological option here. It means that Christians will give up the idea of being in a world apart, which they formerly and

114

rather arbitrarily considered a Christianized world. It means that they remain convinced that Biblical faith, much more than any so-called Christian social doctrine, constitutes a force of invention for the resolving of the problems which a growing economy presents to society. In other words, the task of Christians is not so much to impose a certain order on the world, but to put their own spiritual resources at the service of others, in order to resolve the problems of justice, of peace, of social integration, which arise from the evolution of technological society.

It was this perspective which prevailed in the World Council of Churches Conference on Church and Society (Geneva, 1966) and in the encyclical of Paul VI, *Populorum Progressio,* of March 26, 1967.

This change of perspective had already been sketched out, but less clearly, in the encyclicals of John XXIII (*Mater et Magistra* and *Pacem in Terris*) . The accent of the last encyclical, which is strongly marked by the influence of the French Catholic movement Economie et Humanisme (Lebret is frequently quoted, as are Chenu, de Lubac, and Jacques Maritain) is not much different from preceding encyclicals, which followed the traditional formula in claiming to bring a doctrinal teaching on society. *Populorum Progressio,* on the other hand, is content to analyze the problems of a growing society, to point to the human distress that results from it, and to indicate to Catholics the reasons of faith and the Biblical motivations of their participation "in a concerted action for the integral development of humanity" (Sec. 5) .

In the details of the encyclical, one finds all the themes which had been dealt with by the Conference of Geneva, in particular all those which concern the aid that countries of abundance should give to countries in the process of developing. One finds also the same attention to problems born of the breakup of social structures in the Third World under the shock of an industrialization that has regard neither for man nor for the necessary transitions. One finds the same concern to join social and cultural progress with economic development, the same desire to see an authentic human solidarity become reality beyond ideological, racial, and national barriers ("a more just world and one more structured in a universal solidarity," Sec. 62). Like the Conference of Geneva, Paul VI sees that it is not simply a question of a transfer of material goods, but of a technical assistance aimed at endowing the poorer countries with leadership frameworks, while respecting their autonomy, and also of a concerted action that permits the stabilization of the market price of raw materials. Indeed, this is the permanent cause of that growing imbalance that is noticeable between the two parts of the world: the ample and brutal fluctuations of the market prices do not allow countries whose raw materials are their primary wealth to build a capital that can be invested in modernization. During the last twenty years, Third World countries have raised their exports by 20 percent, but have seen their customs receipts go down by 30 percent because prices dropped faster than production went up.[19] In 1959 and 1960, the price of a North American automobile was the equivalent of twenty sacks of Brazilian coffee. In 1966 it was the equivalent of two hundred and forty sacks of coffee. In these conditions it is difficult for the underdeveloped countries to outfit themselves, and the percentage of the undernourished population continues to grow.

Thus it is extremely pleasant to see that the World Council of Churches and the Roman Catholic Church join voices in calling attention to this catastrophic situation and rediscover together the same prophetic function. It is necessary to rejoice in seeing the Catholic Church part from its long-standing attitude of defending the traditional principles of the social order and to see it thus join the action undertaken by the World Council since 1954. One can only regret that in all conciliar and pontifical documents, the World Council, which has outstripped the Catholic Church, is never mentioned and no mention is made of its work. This is not at all a question of sensitivity. But when all of Christendom is called by the pope himself to take up a service benefiting secular Catholicity, it was surely indicated to mention this convergence.

The pope sees that his proposed lines of action presuppose a calling into question not only of established positions, but even more of social principles which the Catholic Church has long defended. A concerted economy and planning indeed require that the economy no longer have profit as the norm, that free trade no longer be the sole norm of commercial relationships (for in a world in which such a disparity exists between the two parts, free trade can only be a hypocrisy), and that, consequently, private property no longer be considered as an inviolable natural right. In fact, although the encyclical was revised and sugared *in extremis* on this point, it still asserts that "private property does not constitute for anyone an unconditional and absolute right" (Sec. 23) and envisages the possibility of expropriations. Of course, it does not go as far as the Conference of Geneva in its positive appreciation of revolution (Sec. 31), but it is not content to extol a superficial reformism.[20]

Despite all these happy convergences, it is quite certain that divergences still exist in the very fashion of considering the unfolding of history and the relationship between history and eschatology. Human development and full humanism, for both Catholic ethics and Protestant ethics, are surely the objectives which must be proposed to the new civilization. But these objectives are not conceived of in the same way. For Protestant thought they remain ambiguous, marked by the plague of sin. In no way do they signify an access of man to the spiritual maturity of faith. The man who is fully man can remain a rebel against God. For Paul VI, it seems rather that this humanization constitutes the natural base of a supernatural surpassing (and here he seems aware of the thought of Teilhard de Chardin, al-

though he is never quoted) : "Thus human growth constitutes something like a résumé of our duties. Moreover, this
harmony of nature enriched by personal and responsible
effort is called a surpassing. By his insertion into the vivify-
ing Christ, man attains a new blossoming, a transcendent
humanism, which gives him his greatest plenitude" (Sec.
16) . It seems that here we come again across the old theme
of supernature, which comes to crown and fulfill nature.
This impression is even stronger when Paul VI, in a para-
graph in which he emphasizes the ambivalence of human
progress, writes: "The labor of men, and even more for the
Christian, still has the mission of collaborating in the creation of the supernatural world, which is unfinished until
we succeed together in constituting that perfect Man of
which Saint Paul speaks 'who realizes the fullness of
Christ' " (reference to Eph. 4:13) (Sec. 28) . Here we are
in full Teilhardian confusion. The growth of man and his
humanization are confused with the growth toward Christ
and in Christ. A tie of continuity is established between
what the labor of men builds and the Kingdom, between
technical development and the appearance of the new man.
Catholic theology seems thus to take up to its own account
the utopia of a building by man of the Kingdom of God.

An essential difficulty subsists between Catholic and
Protestant ethics, not so much on the level of the concrete
tasks that they indicate, nor on the level of the judgments
that they bring on the conjuncture, but on the level of ultimate motivations. Protestant ethics seeks social justice,
harmonious balance, concerted and interdependent development, because the new man created through faith in
Christ cannot accommodate himself to injustice and because in all human suffering he sees the suffering of Christ.
Catholic ethics certainly does not reject this motivation,
but it adds another to it: by this building of temporal
justice, the Christian allows a natural spiritualization of
man and this spirituality flows by its own movement into
that of Christ. Catholic thought preserves the hope that a

more moral world will necessarily serve as foundation of a believing world. This is why it is persuaded that if Christians knew to ally themselves with non-Christians of good will in order to build a more just and more fraternal world, all men together would come to faith in Christ. The ethical order prepares the way for the eternal order.

We must repeat that a just, fraternal, interdependent world could rise up against God and refuse his grace, just as a world torn by injustice, misery, and war can.

The ethical life of the Christian is a fruit of faith, a free obedience. It is not the condition for entering upon faith. In fact, by its self-sufficiency, it can even close to us the access to faith. The ethical successes of man can be an obstacle to repentance. We must know both that we owe others justice, prosperity, and peace, and that in giving these things to others we do not open to them the doors of the Kingdom. We must drive away poverty and misery, as the God of the gospel expressly commands; yet the same God tells us: "Blessed are the poor."

This paradox was glimpsed at the time of the Reformation, and it remains at the center of the confrontation between Catholic ethics and Protestant ethics.

NOTES

I

1. Martin Luther, *Works,* French edition (Geneva: Labor et Fides), Vol. IX, p. 109.

2. *The Formula of Concord* (Paris: Je Sers, 1948), pp. 165–166.

3. Paul Althaus, *Die Ethik Martin Luthers* (Gütersloh: Gütersloher Verlagshaus Gerd Mohn, 1965). Here we follow Althaus freely.

4. Martin Luther, *Weimarer Ausgabe* 39/1, 46, 28.

5. Here we follow freely the study of François Wendel, *Calvin: Sources et évolution de sa pensée religieuse* (Paris: Presses Universitaires de France, 1950), pp. 182 ff.; English translation, *Calvin: The Origins and Development of His Thought,* by Philip Mairet (Harper & Row, Publishers, Inc.; and London: William Collins Sons & Co., Ltd., 1963).

6. John Calvin, *Opera* 51, 208.

7. John Calvin, *Institutes of the Christian Religion,* tr. by Henry Beveridge (Wm. B. Eerdmans Publishing Company, 1953), III.iii.9.

8. Wendel, *op. cit.,* p. 183

9. John Calvin, Commentary on I Cor. 1:8, Opp. 49/312.

10. *Institutes* III.iii.10.

11. John Calvin, Second Sermon on the Passion, *Opera* 46, 849.

12. *Institutes* III.vi.1.

13. Wendel, *op. cit.,* p. 186.

14. *Institutes* III.xx.42.

15. Wendel, *op. cit.,* p. 187.

16. *Institutes* III.vii.7.

17. *Ibid.,* III.viii.1.

18. André Bieler, *Calvin, prophète de l'ère industrielle* (Geneva: Labor et Fides, 1964).

19. *Institutes* IV.xx.16.

20. M. Grabmann, *Saint Thomas d'Aquin,* French translation by E. Vanstenberghe (Paris: Blond et Gay, 1936), p. 166. We follow freely the work of this author.

21. Grabmann, *ibid.,* p. 169.

22. *Ibid.,* p. 170.

23. *Ibid.,* p. 173.

24. S. Pinckaers, *Le Renouveau de la morale* (Tournai and Paris: Casterman, 1964), pp. 27–28.

25. *Ibid.,* pp. 28–29.

26. *Ibid.,* p. 29.

27. *Dictionnaire de théologie catholique* (Paris: Letouzey et Ané, 1929), Vol. X, 2; second article by Father Dublanchy.

28. *Ibid.,* col. 2396.

29. *Ibid.,* col. 2397.

30. *Ibid.,* col. 2398.

31. The episcopal conference of France (1966) decided to suppress the church laws of the new Catechism.

32. Dublanchy, *loc. cit.,* col. 2398.

33. Paul de Vooght, "Jean Huss au Symposium Hussianum," *Istina,* No. 1 (January–March), 1965–1966, p. 43.

34. For this whole development, see the article by Paul de Vooght.

35. *Catechism for the Use of the Dioceses of France,* published by the Diocese of Clermont (Bourges: André Tardy, 1938), pp. 86–88.

36. To measure the profound transformation taking place in Catholicism it will suffice to compare the Catechism just mentioned with the document published by the plenary conference of the French Episcopacy (*Fonds obligatoire à l'usage des auteurs d'adaptation* [1967]). This document contains theological-pedagogical directions given for the catechism of children from ten to twelve years of age. The chapter on ethics had disappeared completely as an independent chapter. On the

contrary, what is dealt with is the Word of the Risen Christ in our world and of the Holy Spirit, the animator of the Christian life. The moral demands are presented, or rather suggested, on the basis of the work of Christ and of the Holy Spirit. However, the key words are no longer *virtues* or *duties,* but *encounter* (encounter of Christ in the person of the other), *fidelity, generosity, responsibility.* In any case, the concern to root ethics in the Christ event is present throughout.

37. Marc Oraison, *Une Morale pour notre temps* (Paris: Fayard, 1964), especially pp. 55 ff.

38. Text quoted by Oraison, pp. 60–61.

39. *Ibid.,* p. 61.

40. *Ibid.,* pp. 69 and 71.

41. Bernard Häring, *The Law of Christ,* tr. by E. G. Kaiser, 3 vols. (The Newman Press, 1963).

42. Rudolf Schnackenburg, *The Moral Teaching of the New Testament,* tr. by J. Holland-Smith and W. J. O'Hara from the 2d rev. German edition (Herder & Co., 1965).

43. C. Spicq, *Théologie morale du Nouveau Testament,* 2 vols., in the collection *Etudes bibliques* (Paris: Gabalda, 1965).

II

1. In *The Documents of Vatican II* (America Press, 1966), p. 209.

2. Bernard Häring, *La Loi du Christ,* 3 vols. (Fribourg-en-Brisgau, 1954; French translation, Tournai: Desclée et Cie, 1959), Vol. III, p. 23.

3. *Ibid.,* p. 28.

4. *Ibid.,* p. 26.

5. *Ibid.,* p. 27.

6. J. M. Aubert, "Evangile et droit naturel selon l'enseignement de l'Eglise catholique," in the collection *Pratique du droit et conscience chrétienne,* Rencontres No. 64 (Paris: Editions du Cerf, 1962), p. 39.

7. *Ibid.,* pp. 39–40.

8. Emil Brunner, *The Christian Doctrine of Creation and Redemption* (*Dogmatics,* Vol. II), tr. by Olive Wyon (The Westminster Press, 1952), p. 53.

9. *Ibid.*, p. 57.

10. Anders Nygren, *Agape and Eros,* tr. by Philip S. Watson (Harper Torchbooks, Harper & Row, Publishers, Inc., 1969).

11. For a Catholic critique of Nygren's thesis, see the fine work by Mgr. Nédoncelle, *Vers une philosophie de l'amour* (Paris: Aubier, 1946), pp. 23 ff.

12. Aubert, *loc. cit.,* pp. 49–50.

13. *Ibid.*

14. *Ibid.*, p. 55.

15. *Ibid.*, p. 60.

16. This is why, in France, it was necessary to wait until 1950 to see the appearance of the first serious attempt to understand Marxism theologically, in Father H. C. Desroches' *Signification du Marxisme* (Paris: Les Editions Ouvrières). Although the book received the imprimatur, it nevertheless resulted in the expulsion, pure and simple, of the author from the church.

17. Henri Bouillard, *Karl Barth, Parole de Dieu et existence humaine* (Paris: Aubier, 1957), Part II, p. 257. Reference to *Kirchliche Dogmatik,* III/4, pp. 384–385.

18. André Dumas, "La Théologie de Karl Barth et le droit naturel," published in the collective volume, *Pratique du droit et conscience chrétienne.*

19. Karl Barth, *Communauté chrétienne et communauté civile* (2d edition; Geneva: Labor et Fides, 1958), p. 32.

20. *Ibid.*, p. 33.

21. *Ibid.*, p. 41.

22. *Ibid.*

23. *Ibid.*, p. 46.

24. Dumas, *loc. cit.,* pp. 94–95.

25. Dietrich Bonhoeffer, *Letters and Papers from Prison,* ed. by Eberhard Bethge, tr. by Reginald H. Fuller (rev. ed., The Macmillan Company, 1967), pp. 190–191.

26. A. Desqueyrat and M. Halbecq, *L'Enseignement politique de l'église,* Vol. II: *L'Eglise et l'état* (Paris: Spes, 1964), p. 193.

27. "Pastoral Constitution on the Church in the Modern World," Chap. 74, in *The Documents of Vatican II,* p. 284.

28. Jean Daniélou and Jean Bosc, *L'Eglise face au monde* (Paris: La Palatine, 1966), pp. 111–112.

29. *Ibid.*, pp. 98–99.

30. Bonhoeffer, *Letters and Papers from Prison,* pp. 178, 179.

31. See J. P. Gabus, *Introduction à la théologie de la culture de Paul Tillich* (Paris: Presses Universitaires de France, 1969).

32. W. A. Visser 't Hooft, *L'Eglise face au syncrétisme* (Geneva: Labor et Fides, 1964), p. 164.

33. Charles Journet, *La Juridiction de l'église sur la cité* (Paris: Desclée de Brower, 1931), p. 9.

34. Barth, *Communauté chrétienne et communauté civile.*

35. Georges Crespy, *L'Eglise, servante des hommes* (Geneva: Labor et Fides, 1966), pp. 157–158.

36. Karl Barth, *Lettre à un pasteur de la République démocratique allemande,* French translation (Geneva: Labor et Fides, 1959), pp. 48–49.

37. E. Peillaube, "Ame et spiritualité," in *Dictionnaire de théologie catholique,* Vol. I, 1, col. 1021.

38. *Ibid.,* col. 1022.

39. *Ibid.,* col. 791.

40. *Ibid.,* col. 1041.

41. *Ibid.,* col. 1024.

42. H. Mehl-Koehnlein, *L'Homme selon l'apôtre Paul* (Neuchâtel: Delachaux & Niestlé, 1951), p. 26.

43. Häring, *La Loi du Christ,* Vol. III, p. 178.

44. Dietrich Bonhoeffer, *Ethics* (The Macmillan Company, 1955), pp. 112–113.

45. However, it should be noted that this hierarchy is no longer explicitly repeated in the encyclical *Humanae Vitae* and that the two ends of marriage are located on the same level.

46. Bonhoeffer, *Ethics,* p. 113.

47. Rudolf Schnackenburg, *Le Message moral du Nouveau Testament,* French translation (Le Puy and Lyon: Xavier Mappus, 1963), pp. 248–249.

48. *Ibid.,* p. 134.

49. Pinckaers, *op. cit.,* p. 145.

50. *Ibid.,* p. 147.

51. *Ibid.,* p. 149.

52. Häring, *La Loi du Christ,* Vol. I, p. 100.

53. *Ibid.,* p. 321.

54. *Dictionnaire de théologie catholique,* Vol. XII, 2, article on "Sin" by Th. Deman, col. 170.

55. Emmanuel Mounier, *Introduction aux existentialismes* (Paris: Denoël, 1947) , p. 48.

56. R. P. Maydieu, "Nature du péché," in the collective volume *L'Homme et le péché* (Paris: Plon, 1938) , pp. 19 and 21.

III

1. Bonhoeffer, *Letters and Papers from Prison,* pp. 152–153.

2. "Bible et Second Concile du Vatican," in the collective volume *Le Dialogue est ouvert* (Neuchâtel: Delachaux & Niestlé, 1965) .

3. Pinckaers, *op. cit.,* pp. 7–8.

4. Spicq, *op. cit.,* pp. 745–746.

5. Schnackenburg, *op. cit.,* pp. 347–348.

6. Bonhoeffer, *Ethics,* p. 56.

7. Contrary to appearances, the encyclical *Humanae Vitae* has not removed these doubts, since it invites scholars (obviously of a certain persuasion) to pursue their efforts to perfect techniques that, although "natural," are more efficacious because they are authorized.

8. Karl Barth, *Dogmatik* III/4, Part 2, French edition (Geneva: Labor et Fides, 1965) , p. 267.

9. Karl Rahner, *Mission et grâce,* Vol. III: *Au Service des hommes* (Paris: Mame, 1965) , p. 199.

10. Spicq, *op. cit.,* pp. 747 and 750.

11. *Ibid.,* p. 756.

12. *Ibid.,* p. 763.

13. Bonhoeffer, *Ethics,* pp. 17, *et seq.*

14. Spicq, *op. cit.,* p. 763.

15. *Ibid.,* p. 756.

16. *Ibid.,* p. 757.

17. *Ibid.,* p. 758.

18. *Ibid.,* p. 762.

19. André Philip, "Techniques modernes, mutations de structures et valeurs de civilisation," in *Christianisme social,* 74th Year, No. 1–2 (January–February) , 1966.

20. This convergence was shown in 1968 on the occasion of the conference called at Beirut by the Vatican and the World Council of Churches.